MW01182138

MAKING MEMORIES

Celebrating Mothers and Daughters
Through Traditions, Crafts, and Lore

Joyce Marlow

A Fireside Book
Published by Simon & Schuster
New York London Toronto Sydney Singapore

FIRESIDE
Rockefeller Center
1230 Avenue of the Americas
New York, NY 10020

FIRESIDE and colophon are registered trademarks
of Simon & Schuster, Inc.

Designed by Diane Hobbing of Snap-Haus Graphics

Manufactured in the United States of America

10   9   8   7   6   5   4   3   2   1

Library of Congress Cataloging-in-Publication Data
Marlow, Joyce.
    Making memories : celebrating mothers and daughters through
traditions, crafts, and lore / Joyce Marlow.
        p.   cm.
    1. Handicraft.   2. Mothers and daughters—Miscellanea.
3. Mothers and daughters—Anecdotes.   I. Title.

TT145.M37   2001
745.5—dc21   00-066179

ISBN 0-684-87264-1

Acknowledgments

When I asked women to talk about the traditions in their families, I got back stories straight from the heart. They made me laugh, cry, and remember times from my own childhood and that of my daughter. I also gained a new perspective on the relationship between mothers and daughters, and the relevance of traditions that began long ago and still play an important role in our lives. Reading these stories, you can hear the voices of the women who are so much a part of this book and without whom it could not have been written. With their stories came friendship, and for that, too, I am deeply grateful.

Special thanks to my daughter, Heather, for her insights, enthusiasm, and editing skills. One of the best parts of writing this book was getting to relive her childhood through her eyes.

My warmest appreciation to my agent, Maureen Walters, Senior Editors Becky Cabaza and Doris Cooper, Editorial Assistant Claudia Gabel, and the entire team at Simon & Schuster.

For my mother

Contents

MAKING MEMORIES

Introduction

I wrote this book because, as a mother, I wanted to celebrate the many ways in which women weave generations together by passing wisdom and love on to their daughters. I don't think anything adequately prepares a woman for becoming a mother, and especially for the bond she will form with her daughter. The relationship is eternal, no matter the miles between us, how old we grow, or how independent we may believe we are. I think being a mother is the most important job in the world. Although we don't get nearly enough credit for it, the experience is transforming, challenging, and exhilarating.

I believe the reason women find real purpose and value in the symbolic overlays of our lives is that we're grounded in the ongoing processes of life: birth, feeding, growing, nurturing, sheltering, and beyond. Through the practice of teaching what our mothers and grandmothers taught us, we renew traditions and go on to create new ones that complement our lives. Although a mother's biggest challenge might be preparing her daughter to leave her embrace and go out into the world, traditions help us meet this challenge and comprise one of the greatest gifts we both have and are able to give.

When we look at our daughters, we catch a glimpse of ourselves at an earlier, more innocent age. Although traditions aren't always re-creations of the memories of our childhood, that's where they often start. I interviewed more than one hundred women from across the country while writing this book, and found that the same thread of tradition runs through all their lives, as well as mine. Traditions anchor us, add a sense of order and stability, and can identify us and our families like a fingerprint. As the keepers of tradition, women preserve the families of our daughters and granddaughters through the power of knowledge, understanding, skill, artistry, and love.

Traditions don't have to be difficult, time-consuming, or expensive. A tradition might simply be an activity that has brought meaning to your life, one that you want to share with those you love. Maybe you'd like to create new traditions that showcase your special style, or pick up some fresh ideas. Perhaps you didn't have a mother to teach you all that you want to give to your daughter. Here, you'll find tips and suggestions to help you create new traditions to share with your mother and pass along to your daughter.

You only have to use your imagination and energy to make lasting memories and infuse your love and spirit within the generational circle that comprises *family*. I'd also like to encourage you to share your traditions, as well as the memories and the stories that go along with them, with other women. Sisters, nieces, godmothers, cousins, and your very dearest friend—share the essence of your *self* by creating and renewing traditions with each of them.

PART ONE

Making Memories

Chapter 1

Memory Books and Albums

For many women, images from childhood can come rushing back unexpectedly on a quiet sun-glossed morning, while cooking a favorite family recipe, shopping, or just thinking about their children. Usually some stimulus prompts these images. Whether it's sight, sound, or circumstance that triggers these memories, suddenly priceless snapshots in time flood our minds: weddings, christenings, a day at the beach, the birth of a first child, a daughter's sweet sixteen party, or a mother's sixtieth birthday.

Special moments happen throughout our lives—sometimes when we least expect them—and the smallest expressions of love can be the sacred moments we keep close to our hearts. But memories often dim, feelings fade, and in the hustle and bustle of everyday life we tend to forget the things that make us who we are. By sharing our treasured memories with those we love, we form a bond between generations and celebrate our own lives. We can even transform our beloved (but transient) memories into a tangible format that can connect us, both physically and emotionally, to our collective past.

Memory Books and Albums

Memory books and albums are a traditional way to take a nostalgic walk down the streets of your childhood, to remember mothers and grandmothers, and to share their stories with daughters. Better yet, they are easy to create. The first step is deciding what kind of keepsake you want. You might have a theme in mind (a baby book or a wedding album), you might want to use a particular medium (photographs), or you might want to blend mementos, writings, and photos into one book. The choice is yours, and you need only a few basic materials to get started:

- *a large three-ring binder or album*
- *prepunched blank pages*
- *prepunched plastic sleeves*
- *prepunched lined pages for writing notes and remembrances*
- *glue, tape, a stapler, and writing pens*

Memory books and albums allow mothers and daughters to cherish those "firsts" in life. Carol, a friend and author, spent her junior year of college in France. It was an exciting time in her life and her first trip abroad. Her mother kept all the letters and photographs she sent home, put them in an album, and gave the album to Carol when she returned. Carol has delighted in rereading those letters over the years and reliving those memories with her daughter, Nora. Now that Nora is in college, she's keeping alive the tradition started by her grandmother. Nora takes photographs of family gatherings, friends, and special moments, and shares them with friends or family at every opportunity.

I started a scrapbook in seventh grade and kept adding to it until high school graduation. I kept a jumble of things that caught my imagination—interesting newspaper clippings, articles I wrote as editor of my high school newspaper, pressed flowers and corsages that I received from boyfriends, invitations to parties, ticket stubs from movies and theater productions, and photographs of me and my friends. I also kept some pretty unusual items, including a lock of hair from a young man I was sure I'd marry, but didn't.

My daughter, Heather, loves to look through this scrapbook with me. She listens as I retell the stories behind each cherished moment, especially those having to do with her father. He and I met in high school, and quite a few of those pressed flowers came from him. Heather is fascinated by the mementos and stories that chronicled my youth and always has questions. If I'd known how important it was that my daughter learn about my life during those high school years, I'd have written a few sentences about each event or day, and what I was feeling at the time. That extra touch would have really captured the spirit of the past. Unfortunately, those thoughts and feelings have faded with the years and can't be entirely recaptured.

No matter what you keep in your scrapbook or memory album, take the time to add a personal note. If you went shopping for a special occasion (like Christmas or a birthday), include your shopping list, the story of how you found the perfect present, or whether you "shopped till you dropped." If you're in doubt about whether to include something because it doesn't seem important—do it. Whether that something is a "to do" list or a sample from wrapping paper and ribbon, just paste it alongside other mementos. Remember, even the smallest of reminders can trigger the most precious memories.

The first time you take your daughter (or your mother takes you) to the ballet, a musical, or a rock concert, the event is so much more than a program or ticket stub. What happened? Did she love watching the ballerinas twirl or did she fall asleep? Did you go out for lunch at a fancy restaurant? Did she try pâté or escargot for the first time? Those "firsts" in life are so precious, be sure and capture them for all time.

Photograph Album

If you're like most people, your photographs are in a drawer rather than a photo album. The chore of organizing pictures always gets pushed to the bottom of the list, right under cleaning the bedroom closet. Unfortunately, time can dim the depth of the emotions of the day and the "feel-good" stories and amusing anecdotes our daughters would enjoy hearing from us when they're older.

Old-Fashioned Cocoa

4 heaping teaspoons sugar
2 heaping teaspoons baking
  cocoa
2 cups milk
½ teaspoon real vanilla
miniature marshmallows or
  whipped cream

Stir sugar and cocoa together in small saucepan. Gradually stir in ¼ cup milk to make a smooth paste. Stir in remaining milk and warm over medium heat, stirring constantly until hot. Remove from heat, stir in vanilla, and pour into mugs. Float miniature marshmallows or whipped cream on top and enjoy!
Makes two servings.

With that thought comes an idea for a wonderful rainy day tradition. Make steaming hot cocoa the old-fashioned way, pop a marshmallow or two into each cup, pull out that box of photos, and walk down memory lane with your mother or daughter.

Here are a few tips to get you started with a photo album:

- *Write a "memory note" on the back of each photo (and in the album).*
- *Organize and label photos by date or occasion.*
- *Start with the last time you took photos (instead of starting with the oldest photos) so you won't be overwhelmed.*

Recipe Book

Many of our warmest memories are associated with preparing meals for our families, whether cooking old family recipes, creating something new and fun, or setting a beautiful table with china and silver. Another type of memory book comes from Pat, a lifelong midwesterner. When Pat's three daughters were growing up, each one had favorite foods and meals. As the girls grew older, Pat looked ahead to the day they would leave home and made a separate (and very special) recipe book for each daughter. When the girls moved out on their own, Pat started inviting them for Sunday morning brunches featuring their favorite recipes. One thing led to another, and the girls pitched in with the cooking and ended up spending half the day with their mother. Pat's ingenuity started two traditions—the recipe books *and* Sunday brunches.

You can start a family recipe book by collecting recipes from the cooks in your family. This could get tricky because some cooks measure by "a pinch" or "a handful" rather than "a teaspoon" or "a tablespoon." One way to manage this problem is to watch that favorite dish being prepared. That way, you can write everything down and visit at the same time. If you're the keeper of family recipes, be sure to record measurements and directions as well as any special cooking tips. Write out the recipe by hand and paste it in your recipe album—alongside a shopping list for the needed ingredients.

I would also encourage you to write a few notes about each recipe—not just that it tastes great but that it was your sister's favorite dish or that you usually serve it for holidays, Dad's poker nights, or the kids' sleep overs. Recipes handed down from your mother and grandmother should be included, especially if they were written by hand, along with a few lines about entertaining and why food is so much a part of your family gatherings.

Wedding Albums

Wedding albums are something most women keep, but here's an innovative idea. Iris held a special scrapbook wedding shower for her daughter, Jennifer, and her fiancé, Rob, and asked family and childhood friends to bring photos of the couple when they were growing up. As you might imagine, some were flattering, while others showed a mischievous and even outrageous side to both the future bride and her groom. Iris pasted the photos in an album and asked the guests to jot down a few sentences to accompany each one. Then guests took turns retelling stories that were sometimes warm and affectionate and other times funny and embarrassing.

When you can appreciate both the adversities and accomplishments someone experiences in childhood, you come closer to understanding the adult. Jennifer and Rob learned a lot about each other that night with the help of family and friends who created a memory album documenting their lives from childhood up to the wedding. A person's story might begin at birth, and a woman's wedding day might be "the most important day in her life," but since there's so much more to our history and heritage than the monumental events, "every day" albums can commemorate the daily beauty in all our lives.

Summer Memory Book

You can start a summer memory album on the last day of any school year, whether you're in fifth grade or college. When school ended, I always had extravagant plans for the summer. I was going to read the classics, take up a hobby, learn how to sew or paint, lose ten pounds, swing dance, plant a garden, and a zillion other things. All these thoughts, words, and deeds should be in your summer memory book.

Dorothy has a monthly traditional "picnic day" during the summer with her daughter, Amy. They spend the morning getting lunch ready and making a special dessert. Sometimes it's cupcakes, but usually they stick to cookies because they're easy to make and pack. You could even buy cookie dough in the refrigerated section of the grocery store so all you have to do is slice and bake. Dorothy and Amy usually go to a city park for their picnic, but there's no reason you can't take a leisurely drive to the countryside.

Summer Picnic Fun

Pack sandwiches, fruit, cookies, and bottled water. Take along a Frisbee; a baseball glove, ball, and bat; a jump rope; or other athletic equipment. Take a good book to share and an old blanket to spread on the ground. Wear shoes suitable for running or climbing and have fun!

When my daughter was quite small, we had summer picnics at the nearby grade school playground. That gave me the perfect opportunity to be a kid, too, and play on the swings and jungle gym with the excuse that I was playing with my daughter. Although I did take a few photos of our picnic traditions, like so many mothers who have grown children, I wish I had more tangible reminders of those days.

We had another favorite outing—weekend campouts at New Brighton Beach (near Santa Cruz, California) with one idea in mind: relaxation and fun. We'd bury each other in the sand, swim and play in the surf, walk along the shore looking for shells and pretty driftwood to take home, or toss a Frisbee. I got in plenty of reading time, too, sunning myself while watching Heather; her brother, Brian; and the occasional playmate who came along. Outings like this are perfect opportunities to create summer memory books. They also give you a way to spend time with your children doing something you all enjoy.

Another hallmark of summer is a vacation, whether it's the one you've been planning forever or a spur-of-the-moment getaway. Add maps, tickets from sightseeing adventures, postcards, and personal observations, and you've got something to keep and share with your daughter or mother.

School Memory Book

School days are filled with memories that can be lost over time if we aren't careful to keep them close to our hearts. Barbara, the author of over thirty romance novels, started a school memory book for each of her daughters. These books provide a veritable history of each child, including report cards, honors, awards, term papers, artwork, programs of events the girls took part in, and other remembrances of childhood. What a great way to foster self-esteem in your daughters—by celebrating and remembering their victories, no matter how great or small.

Theme Memory Book

You can make theme memory books for any special occasion or interest. Holidays that include family celebrations are a good place to begin, especially Thanksgiving, Christmas, New Year's Eve, Independence Day, and Halloween. These holidays are filled with family get-togethers and traditional festivities. You could create a memory book that highlights one holiday over several years, or one that includes all the holidays for a particular year. Include photographs, mementos, entertaining tips, guest lists, amusing stories, and special highlights.

Another great idea for a theme memory album is the seasons of the year—spring, summer, fall, and winter. This project is especially interesting for anyone who loves nature and the outdoors. Capture the beauty of the natural world by pressing flowers and leaves from the garden. Once the cuttings are dry, slip them into plastic sleeves along with a description, a note telling where and when you found them, and an explanation of what each cutting means to you. Add favorite poems or sayings about each season, or try writing a few of your own. Include photos and information about different species that interest you—butterflies, bees, birds, insects, and mammals—their habits, and their natural habitats.

On the lighter side, there's always kitchen artwork. Mothers cherish the scribbled drawings children bring home from school, and post them with pride on the refrigerator. When putting up your pint-sized Picasso's new masterpiece, save the older "classics" for an album called "Best Refrigerator Art of the Year."

If your daughter is involved in sports, cheerleading, the school newspaper, or any number of extracurricular activities, you might have enough material to fill a theme album. My daughter was in Job's Daughters (a Christian organization for girls ages twelve to eighteen who are of Masonic heritage) when she was a teenager. The Masons have been around for generations and are committed to serving the community and those with special needs. Over the years, Heather held a variety of positions, became an officer, and eventually led the group. She was active in so many social, service, and charitable activities that we were able to fill two albums.

Traditions don't necessarily have to start when your daughter is young. Adele, an administrative manager in California, took tradition *up* the generational ladder by making "growing-up" albums for both her grandmothers. She spent time with each of them and traced memories from childhood and beyond, so she could fill in the blanks and get to know what her grandmothers were like as children. She helped them collect photos, cards, memories, and family history and put it all together in albums that Adele will share with her own daughter one day.

If you decide to make this kind of album, ask your grandmothers to write about their childhoods, parents, school days, weddings, holidays, and favorite things. Be sure and give them nice stationery or parchment paper to write on so that you can imitate the antique look of old tattered letters in museums that evoke such wonderful memories of the past. My mother has several letters written by my ancestors, including one from my great-grandfather proposing marriage to my future great-grandmother. If your family has letters like this, be sure to include them in your album.

Videos and Audiotapes

Filmmaking shouldn't be reserved for professionals—why not include videos when capturing your family memories? I can't think of a more perfect way to capture a story about how Grandpa proposed to Grandma than having her tell it in her own words. Before asking your grandmother or mother to participate, research techniques used in filming, indoor and outdoor lighting, angles, film, cameras, and audio equipment and techniques. You will find plenty of resources at your library or on the Internet.

If you don't have video equipment, do an audio interview of two, three, or four generations of mothers and daughters. In either case, spend time together before turning on the camera or tape recorder so everyone will feel relaxed and comfortable. Then focus your thoughts on the past and talk about anything and everything that comes to mind, special and everyday events, a particular topic, or just girl talk. It's a good idea to have a list of questions to ask, and I'd suggest giving them to participants ahead of time so they can prepare. I'd also let participants know that these are only preliminary questions, because others are sure to come up during the taping. You don't want to miss out on a great story by being limited by the list. Here are a few topics and questions that might lead you in the right direction:

- *Discuss your childhood and teenage years, where you lived and went to school, your interests, and your hobbies.*
- *Describe how your husband proposed, your wedding ceremony, what you and the bridesmaids wore, the reception, and the honeymoon.*
- *What surprised you about being married? What were the hardest adjustments to make?*
- *Talk about each of your children and what makes them different and special.*
- *What is your greatest joy or your greatest sorrow?*
- *Were you close to your grandmother? Describe your relationship with her and your favorite memories.*
- *Reminisce about a favorite childhood Christmas, birthday, and Mother's Day.*
- *Describe how your mother celebrated family traditions at holidays, which traditions you follow, and which you celebrate differently.*
- *What interests, talents, and skills did your mother or grandmother hand down to you (such as cooking, sewing, quilting, gardening, nature walks, music, and art)?*
- *What is the best and worst thing that ever happened to you?*

When you make a videotape or audiotape, give copies to everyone who participated, as well as to your closest relatives, so that these stories will be preserved for the future.

Memories on the Internet

It seems as if the old tradition of memory albums and scrapbooks is being partially replaced by personal web pages on the Internet. Although personal web pages are a new and interesting medium, you need to be aware of some pitfalls. The Internet tends to be fluid, in that web pages are generally updated from time to time. That means losing older data and images, and that could prove costly in terms of history. When you update your web pages, don't replace information if you want your children (and their children) to relive your memories and share in family traditions. Instead, continually add to your web site to create an endless chronicle of personal stories, memories, scanned photographs, and images.

Keep in Mind

When creating memories:
- *Find something you have in common with your daughter—a hobby, sport, place, or activity—and start a scrap or memory book together. Sharing both the activity and making the album will give you the opportunity to spend time together doing something you both enjoy.*
- *Keep searching for unique ways to display your memories—for instance, take all those photos, children's artwork, theater programs, even Grandma's favorite recipes, and create a collage and frame it, or make a decoupage and cover a box meant for saving keepsakes. Remember, never use the original; use a copy instead.*

Chapter 2

Journals, Diaries, and Genealogy

*A*lmost everyone has kept a diary or journal at some time. Whether the writer's purpose is keeping track of daily activities, expressing feelings, or contemplating the future, journals and diaries should be intimate and uninhibited. In their purest form, diaries and journals serve as private confessionals where we write from the heart, uncensored and fearless. We don't worry about grammar or fumble for a precise word or phrase. We simply put pen to paper and write whatever it is we want to remember next week or years from now.

Thoughts that are hidden away in diaries and journals can be both revealing and insightful. Once you've kept a diary for a year or two, you might begin to recognize patterns in your life touching on relationships, career, family, or personal successes or failures. A journal spanning the first few years of marriage might reveal ways in which two people successfully blend their lives. Entries exploring the difficulties of a career choice, raising toddlers or teenagers, or overcoming a handicap or health problem disclose a lot about a person's inner strengths and weaknesses.

You should consider whether you want your daughter to read your journal. After all, when we write with no holds barred, all kinds of things come up, and not all of them are pretty. I use my journal as a sounding board to vent my fears and frustrations, and to rant about injustices (real or imagined), as well as to work out inner struggles. It's of great value to me, and one day may help my daughter understand that I never had all the answers, but that I always struggled to find them.

Terry, a graphic designer and quilt enthusiast, has her mother's handwritten account of her life, including many happy memories. But for Terry, the most important passages are the ones that provide a stark look at her mother's character. During the depression of the 1930s, she lived in the Dust Bowl of the Great Plains. One image that stayed in Terry's mind is how her mother slept with a wet cloth over her face to keep the dust out of her lungs. Despite the hardships, Terry's mother wrote about good times, too. She chronicled family stories through the years and expressed the love she felt for the grandmother she called "my angel" and who traveled west on the Oregon Trail.

Terry's mother wrote a dedication inside the front cover of her journal: "These remembrances are for my children and grandchildren. I hope you will find them interesting." When Terry told me the story of her mother, she mentioned that she hadn't touched her quilting for months but now saw it "not only as important for me, but someday it may be meaningful in ways I never before considered." As you can see, journals and diaries can help you think about the legacy you've received from your mother and the one you're leaving behind.

When Fran, a novelist, read the diaries her mother kept during eleven of the most pivotal years of her life, it wasn't the historical value that interested her. "It was her personal reaction to the things that happened to her. Mostly, though, I was struck by her cheer, compassion, and incredible courage in the face of tragedies. But my mother didn't just write about the hard times. When she met my father at a dance on July 16, 1938, she wrote in her journal that it was a 'Red Letter Day in My Life.'

"They didn't marry for five years, so I was privy to the ups and downs of their courtship. They broke up for almost a year because she caught him with another woman ('a Catholic girl,' my mother wrote), and she agonized over it for several weeks until my father swore off other women forever and they got back together. When my father went to Texas to study navigation with the air force, she sent him cards and letters (which I still have) telling him how proud she was to wear his wings when she went out with her war plant co-workers. However, everything wasn't perfect. My father's mother gave her grief because she was a Methodist, and my mother debated about whether or not to convert. But in 1943, my mother ended her journal with one final word—'Married!' and ended her diaries there."

By reading these journal passages, Fran learned about her mother through her own words. Although Fran isn't sure why her mother stopped writing in her diary, she does know that the early years of her parents' marriage were difficult and marked by change.

History suggests that women have written more journals and diaries than men during the last century. Women's diaries began as laundry lists of domestic chores, linens, and food for the pantry. Over time, we started including details about daily life, our families, and our environment. Finally, women's journals became a written legacy of our most intimate hopes, fears, and desires, and a history of our families' fortunes and misfortunes.

Louisa May Alcott wrote her novel *Little Women* from the pages of her childhood journal, and Anne Frank inspired generations with the diary she wrote during World War II. Just think of the differences you'd expect to find in the diaries of a twelve-year-old girl, a young woman of twenty, a new mother, and, finally, a grandmother. If you read a journal of one woman that spanned all those years, you would get to know her very well.

It's not only women of past generations who have kept journals. Today many women find time in their busy lives to write down their thoughts and feelings. I've heard Oprah Winfrey say she started keeping a diary when she was a teenager and that she continues that tradition today. Oprah might have started out with the idea of writing for a few minutes each day, but she has created an intimate memoir of her life that spans thirty years.

I think most of us are interested in how our mothers felt about their lives, the people they grew up with, and the families they loved. We are, after all, products of our childhoods. Knowing how a person was reared, where and how he or she lived, and the stories of those he or she loved helps us understand that person today. In the case of mothers and daughters, I think journals and diaries provide us with a chance to *know* each other in the deepest sense of the word.

Getting Started

If you're interested in writing but don't have the time to write every day, start with once a week. Find some quiet, reflective time and write by hand in a beautiful journal. The easiest way to begin is to recall the week's events. As you explore your activities, thoughts, and feelings, write about everything that comes to mind. Here are a few questions that might spark your creativity:

- *How did you feel when you woke this morning and why?*
- *What are your goals for the week? The year? If you don't have any, make a list of ambitions that are important to you.*
- *What happened today (or this week) that brought you joy or made you sad?*
- *Choose a birthday or holiday from the past and write down everything you can remember about the day.*
- *If you could have anything you wanted, what would it be and why?*

One of the best things about diaries is that you can go back and reread them to better understand the path your life has taken and to gain insights into the journey ahead. When I turned thirteen, my mother gave me my first diary, a small white padded book with pink hearts on the cover. It closed with a tiny lock and key. I just loved to write in it. When I grew older, though, I replaced my girlhood diary with lined, bound journals that contained more mature observations about my life. Here's an entry from just before my wedding day:

July 14th. Two more days until the wedding and counting. I'm really nervous and scared. And I don't know what to do with my feelings. Len doesn't understand—he doesn't see anything to be nervous about—so why do I have all these feelings crawling in my stomach? It's so over the top I just want to run away. Where, I don't know, or even why, except that it's too much to deal with. I wanted a simple dress, a simple ceremony, but Mom wanted me to have a "real" wedding. She's been working on my dress for weeks—white satin, lace, and twenty little covered buttons on the back. I feel like everyone is taking over my life and I'm not even here anymore. I'm somewhere and somebody else.

I think it's pretty common to have prewedding jitters, no matter how much in love you are. At the time, I'm sure I thought the feeling of not being there was pretty unusual, but I don't imagine it is. Like Fran's mother, when I married and had children my journal entries dwindled and then ceased for a number of years, but even those scant entries have given me insights into the patterns of my life.

Computer Journals

About ten years ago, I started keeping my journal on a computer. Although you lose the personal touch of handwriting, you gain the ease of a keyboard, the speed of typing, and the ability to include copies of E-mails and other electronic information from the Internet. Take Ruth, for example. Even though her family is spread across the country, Ruth stays connected to relatives through E-mail. "There is more written communication between our family members than ever. With a PC in every home, we can touch base with each other regularly or send electronic birthday cards when we've forgotten to put one in the mailbox."

Family Newsletters

Pat and her family moved to Michigan when she was thirteen. That's when her mother started writing a newsletter and sending it to her sisters to keep in touch. After Pat got married, at age twenty-one, she continued the tradition by sending a newsletter to her mother, and when her own daughters were grown, she gave them a compilation of all those letters chronicling their childhood, including the originals that her mother had created.

Before you start your own family newsletter, you have a few decisions to make:

- *Do you write everything yourself or ask other family members to contribute?*
- *Do you tell only the good news or include the not-so-good, such as serious illnesses, employment reverses, low scores in school, and so forth?*
- *Should those "appearing in print" have the right to change or veto what you've written about them?*
- *How many times a year will the newsletter come out? Quarterly, monthly, or when enough has happened (or that you want to talk about) that you have enough material to fill a page or two?*
- *Will you publish the newsletter in print or on the Internet?*

The last question is especially important, considering how diverse our means of communication have become. If you think the Internet is too unconventional, keep in mind that family newsletters can be just as personal in cyberspace as they are on paper. Michelle has a business managing web sites on the Internet, and she thinks it's the perfect place for her display of family photos, favorite poems, and her own family newsletter. "Since so many of us have spread ourselves out around the world, our newsletter on the web keeps us informed. We receive news about friends, get links to other places of interest, and find out what's happening in each other's lives." Michelle invites you to check out her family newsletter at www.myownassistant/personal/personal.htm.

Genealogy

Over the last decade, old family letters, journals, and Bibles have sparked a renewed interest in genealogy. If you're interested in your family tree but aren't ready for a huge project, try starting with what you know. Getting started isn't nearly as difficult as you might think.

- *Write down everything you know about your immediate family, including dates and places of birth, marriage, and so on. Do the same thing for your parents, grandparents, and as far back as you can, using one sheet of paper for each family.*
- *Once you have these notes, sit down with your mother or oldest living relative and see if you can fill in the blanks.*
- *Consider taking along a tape recorder so you can visit and ask questions instead of having to focus on taking notes.*
- *Ask your relatives if you can look at any old Bibles, letters, photographs, newspaper clippings, birth records, and marriage certificates.*
- *If you've caught the genealogy bug in earnest, the next step is to search external sources such as the county courthouse, the U.S. Census Bureau, ship manifests, newspaper archives, and obituaries.*
- *Many of these records, as well as genealogy research*

sites, can now be accessed on the Internet. Here are a few to start with:

The Church of Latter-day Saints has one of the most extensive genealogical archival sites in the world. If you can't visit its research facility in Salt Lake City, Utah, its web site is www.familysearch.org.

Cyndi's List is a personal genealogical site with over 61,000 links to take you to a world of information, including research tools; U.S. Census records; military, history, religious, and locality sites; as well as information for those who have been adopted. The web site is www.CyndisList.com.

Another comprehensive, personal web site with over 70,000 links can be found at www.genealogy toolbox.com.

Kelly, who enjoys fishing and renovating her hundred-year-old home, became interested in her family history when her mother gave her a family Bible with an old document folded inside. "Growing up, my mother and I were not close at all. I was always my dad's favorite. When I was twelve, they divorced, and Mom moved us halfway across the country. Later, she remarried, and that's when things went from bad to worse and I made the personal decision to distance myself from her. I was married with my own children when Mom gave me the Bible. She knew I was interested in genealogy, and although she couldn't say the things I needed to hear, giving me her personal heirlooms felt like an expression of approval. She reached out to me in a way she'd never done before, and it was one of the things that helped bring us closer. After reading this old family history document, which had come from my great-grandmother, I decided to pursue all of my family branches and see what I could come up with. The Internet made it much easier.

"Shortly after I began the project, a great-aunt passed away. My mother asked me to go to the funeral with her because she thought it would give me an opportunity to visit my great-aunts and gather information. That little trip brought us closer than we have ever been—we laughed, cried, and shared things that we never had before. It's interesting that what brought us together after all these years had been there all the time—family history. It just took the spark of an old letter from my great-grandmother to her descendants to jump-start our relationship and allow the progression of a lifetime and all the tiny threads that formed the final piece to come together."

Indeed, with the advent of the Internet, genealogy research is becoming easier all the time. Lorrie, a technical writer and computer hobbyist, found researching her Oregon lineage a long-distance challenge, but the availability of the Internet made many of the seemingly impossible tasks incredibly fast and easy. Lorrie also met many people on the Internet who shared her passion for genealogy and acted as a unique support system that helped her achieve her goals.

I, too, was using the Internet as a research tool when I discovered Lorrie's web site at www.members.home.net/lvtree. She uses the site to share stories and letters written by her ancestors, especially Sarah, her great-great-grandmother. Lorrie's interest in genealogy started when she inherited a small box of Sarah's old letters that had been passed down through the generations. For Lorrie: "As I read through those writings of day-to-day life, I began to get a feel for how life was one hundred years ago. I've never been much of a history buff, but somehow these letters made it all seem so personal and intimate. It was as though my great-great-grandmother had reached out across all those generations and laid a gentle hand on my heart." Here's a passage from one of those letters:

Arlington, Oregon. Thurs, Feb 6, 1902.
Dear Mother. . . . The children are nearly sick with bad colds and the baby is cutting teeth and is a little cross. She has two and two

more nearly through. She is sitting alone and is trying to creep. I got yours and Daisy's letter a few days ago and my, was I surprised to get the pictures. Soon as good weather comes, I am going to have the baby's pictures and will send you one. It has been cold here. 12 degrees below zero and . . . I tell you, I don't want to be where it is any colder. . . . I am rocking the cradle and writing on my lap. I doubt if you can read this at all!

Diaries, journals, letters, and other genealogical artifacts will provide you with new connections to generations of your female ancestors. Add your own voice to this lineage by keeping a journal and recording the events of your life. Collect and keep family letters for their sentiment, their value as history, and as a genealogical research tool. Here are some other ways to ensure that your family history spans generations:

- *Go on a photographic treasure hunt in search of your women forebears. Look among old boxes in the attic. When you visit your grandmother, take another look at the*

Journal Book Covers

Con-Tact paper, preglued wallpaper, or soft leather
2 pieces cardboard or matboard, 6″ × 9″ or 9″ × 12″
Good-quality paper, lined or unlined, 5½″ × 7″ or 8½″ × 11″, for journal pages
PVA glue or Yes! glue
1-hole or 3-hole punch
1 yard cord or raffia
Beads with large enough hole to string on cord or raffia

Cut Con-Tact paper, preglued wallpaper, or soft leather 3″ larger all around than the pieces of matboard or cardboard. Set board on top, centering so the excess is even. Fold the top edge down and the bottom edge up, making neat corners, and press inward with your hands. Fold the sides neatly around board (if using leather, first apply glue around the edges of the leather). Punch holes in covers (and paper if not prepunched) and line up. Thread cord or raffia through the top hole, around the back, then up through the bottom hole. Tie a knot, slip beads on each strand and keep in place by tying another knot.

mantel or hallway walls, check the bureau where a great-aunt keeps old linens, the pages of ancient albums and books, the box where your grandfather kept his cuff links and watch, or even his old wooden cigar box.

- *Have a taped interview with your mother to discover and record her life <u>before</u> you were part of it.*
- *If you enjoy crafts, make your own unique journal.*
- *Continue the tradition by giving your daughter (no matter what her age) a daily diary with a design that compliments her personality.*
- *Create a family tree with your mother or daughter as the focus at the base of the tree. You could start with the standard design of a tree with branches, use an opened fan as a motif, or use a diagram with tiers for different generations. For a historical look, try calligraphy on ecru-colored handmade paper, or thick black ink on white parchment paper. Put together a portrait tree using a handful of family photographs on a mat with multiple openings. Add a nice frame and you're finished in an afternoon.*
- *Make a generational booklet with both photos and text. Separate your family into chapters (whether the booklet is focused on the women in the family, sisters, or one generation), writing a sentence or two about each person or family, including birthdays, weddings, special talents or interests, and a little information about where they live. Print the pages, have them copied on 11″ × 7″ paper (two-sided, like a book), staple them in the middle, and fold. Select a nice cover and paste a photo on the front.*

Heirlooms and Keepsakes

have a small beaded handbag that belonged to my grandmother. She gave it to my mother, who gave it to me. The handbag is worn, the colors have muted with the years, and some beads are missing. Still, it is one of my prized possessions. When I glance at the bag, framed on a background of watered silk and hanging in my living room next to two gilt-edged saucers from my daughter, I find comfort in the link between generations of women in my family.

Heirlooms and keepsakes weave memories, love, and tradition into a seamless pattern that ties generations of daughters together. The things we call heirlooms come in all shapes, sizes, and types. They generally have a monetary value as well as family history. The paintings and jewelry my mother brought back from India and Vietnam during her world travels, the silver tea service passed down from my great-great-grandmother, and my grandmother's wedding ring and her elaborately carved walnut rocking chair are my most cherished heirlooms. Keepsakes, though, are small mementos or tokens that have great sentimental value but little monetary importance. Keepsakes I've collected over the years include the costume jewelry my mother let me play with as a child, a tiny cedar box that belonged to my grandmother, and the silver thimble my mother wore when she hemmed my skirts.

Made by Hand

Heirlooms and keepsakes made by hand have special significance because there is something of the *person* imbued within the item itself. My mother was a painter, usually of small landscapes, and my daughter is an artist who works with mixed media. My artistic skill comes out in textiles. The pieces that come from this tradition of expressing creativity through our hands surely carry something of each of us within them.

Cindy inherited a handmade chest her great-great-grandfather made for his daughter when she got married at the respectable age of fourteen. "You can still see the tongue-and-groove work and the square-headed nails. The pine chest was a dowry or wedding gift and was passed down through generations of daughters within the family. I remember that my grandmother kept the chest in her basement, filled with quilt tops her mother had pieced but never finished. I feel proud when I look at the chest, because it reminds me of my great-great-grandmother's struggles, and it's this sense of pride that I'd like to pass on to my daughter—along with the chest and pictures of most of the women who have owned the chest."

Terry, unfortunately, had the sad duty of sorting out her mother's possessions after she passed away: "As I began to list the items in my parents' home, I started focusing on the art—my father's carvings, my mother's paintings, drawings, and pottery. She had left something made by my parents or grandparents' hands to various relatives in order to carry their voices into the future. Never before had it struck me how these objects are actually a part of my mother and what a powerful influence they have been in my life."

Terry makes an excellent point—it's not just the silver or china that we cherish, but the glimpse into the past that we inherit along with the tangible.

Books and Papers

When I was growing up, my mother used *The American Woman Cookbook,* a basic, home-style cookbook that her mother had given her when she was first married. I loved it so much, my mom found a used copy and gave it to me when I was a newlywed. Many years later, my mother and I came across another used copy in a bookstore. I snatched it up and gave it to my daughter, who has the same kinds of memories about this book as I did. What wonderful memories it conjured up for all of us.

For Joanne: "Some of my most prized possessions aren't the jewelry, crystal, or china, but letters written to my great grand-mother, Margaret Leonora, from her mother-in-law, Rachael. They were written on anniversaries or birthdays, and in them she thanked Margaret for being such a wonderful wife to her son and for being such a wonderful daughter to her. I also have Rachael's last will and testament, in which she lists things almost item-by-item, talking about the love she had for her son, William, her daughter, Grace, and her daughter-in-law, Margaret. My grandmother wrote two letters to me to be opened after she died. In them, she wrote with the same love that her grandmother had so many years before. She explained about her funeral arrangements, talked about her feelings toward me, and gave me detailed information on all the heirlooms she had, who they had belonged to before her, what they were used for, when they were used, etc."

Joanne's great-great-grandmother wanted family connections and history preserved, and she did it by putting pen to paper. Here are a few ways we can do the same:

- *Make a list of your heirlooms and their history. Include more than just names and dates—memorialize whatever stories you have about who gave what to whom, when, and on what occasion.*
- *Write a letter communicating your wishes as to who should inherit your heirlooms and keepsakes. Even if*

not included in a Last Will and Testament, this letter can serve as a guide for your family.

- *Write a letter to your mother and daughter every year on their birthdays, reminiscing about the past and rekindling your relationships. Urge them to keep the letters so they can be passed on as keepsakes to the generations of women to come.*

Silver, China, and Crystal

Kelly, a writer and poet, has her great-grandmother's silver and some crystal pieces from her father's mother to pass on to her two daughters. For Kelly: "I believe more than ever that our love carries on in the personal things we leave behind. The things I treasure most in my life (besides my children, husband, and family) are the things that belonged to my mother, grandmothers, and great-grandparents. It's those things that bring them to life and make them more than just names on a genealogical chart."

Joanne was lucky enough to start receiving heirlooms from her mother and grandmother at an early age: "My grandmother saw my interest in family heirlooms and started giving me different things as gifts when I turned thirteen. For special occasions or birthdays it would be a ring, a pendant, or a piece of crystal. By the time I was twenty-one and getting married, I had quite a collection. I'll never forget the look on my grandmother's face that first Christmas when I had the whole family over for Christmas dinner and actually used some of the china that had been handed down to me. I'm continuing a family tradition by starting to pass things along to my daughter, Jackie, when she turned thirteen."

If you've inherited incomplete place settings of china, silver, or crystal, you can still create a beautiful table. For china, use the main theme (florals or gold rims, for example) or color of the china as a guide to help you find pieces at secondhand or antiques shops to fill in the gaps. For crystal and silver, look for pieces very different from what you have, so there's no mistaking this "mis-matched" look was done by design.

How to Use Your Heirlooms Every Day

Joanne doesn't believe in keeping her heirlooms in display cabinets. "I guess out of all the keepsakes, one of my favorites is a plain white coffeepot that was brought over from Germany and used for the first time at my great-grandmother's christening in 1878. I do keep that piece in the china cabinet, but often use my beautiful set of Victorian berry bowls for fruit desserts. I also use a cut-glass water pitcher and vases for flowers throughout the year, since my husband loves to bring home flowers. Assorted sizes of cut-glass dishes make great candy dishes and hold small candles or ornaments at Christmas. I use the Victorian and cut-glass sugar and creamers at various times when we have company, and use all the handmade doilies and tablecloths throughout the year.

"I also have two quilts that have been passed down, and I use them to cover older dressers, with a small doily on top to protect them. My mother-in-law gave me a beat-up old tarnished pewter water pitcher (with apologies for its condition). It has the lid attached, so I just open it, leave the lid up, and arrange a spray of dried and silk flowers. I have several photo albums and large pictures from the early 1900s, and christening gowns from my great-grandfathers and -grandmothers. I plan to set up a 'family wall' and hang all the large pictures and the christening gowns in a hall or staircase."

A New Generation

There are many traditions to celebrate and heirlooms, both new and old, to pass down at the birth of a new baby—christening gowns, satin or silk embroidered booties, silver christening cups engraved with the baby's name, crib coverlets made with fine linen and laces, cradles, and a rocking chair for Mom.

Jill, a real estate broker in her early thirties, had her first child last year. She'd been hoping for a daughter and got just what she wanted—eight-pound, red-haired Abigail. "A few weeks after I told my family the good news, they started sending me heirlooms. My mom sent the little gold locket she'd bought for my christening, and my great-aunt passed on the silver rattle she'd had as a child. She didn't have children, and was pleased to give it to Abigail. When I opened each of these gifts, I felt an affinity to the past and a sense that I was continuing an important family legacy."

Rose has four children, and she and her husband, Harold, are welcoming their grandchildren with heirlooms. "Harold brought the cradle in last night—it's finished! The wood is cherry, and after several coats of tung oil, it glows, and will deepen in color with age. Heidi has been waiting for a baby for years and had about given up hope, so this baby is a real treasure. Each of our four children will receive a cradle for their firstborn, to be passed down through their families and used for generations to come."

Cindy, a stay-at-home mom, sums up my feelings about heirlooms and keepsakes: "One of the greatest rewards of growing older is having your grown children surprise you with the special memories they have nurtured and cherished all their lives. In a world of uncertainty, continuity within the family can be reassuring, giving all of us a feeling of security and love."

Unique Collections

Mary Jo, a writer raised on a farm in upstate New York, grew up dreaming of China. "My mother, Eleanor Congdon Putney, lived in China as a child because her father taught at the Peking medical school. Even decades later, my mother's memories are crystal clear, and she remembers some of the Mandarin she learned. In fact, because children pick up language so much more easily than adults, she functioned as her mother's translator. My mother's Chinese collection had been gathered by my grandmother and consisted of gorgeous embroidered silk garments, shining brass teapots, an opium water pipe, carved jade, and other exotic treasures that were part of my children's world. I had a particular fondness for a small perfume bottle carved from rock crystal with an elegant goldfish painted on the inside.

"Since my mother now lives in a small apartment, some of her collection resides with me. When I started my historical romance *The China Bride,* I unpacked these treasures to remind myself of the richness and power of Chinese objects. There is a particular scent that goes with very old silk that was exactly as I remembered from my childhood. To provide inspiration for the writing, I took a small embroidered panel rich with Taoist symbols and a white jade pendant up to my computer room so I could see and touch them as I worked. I've never been to China, but because of my mother, I can still dream of it."

I've been able to see places through my mother, too. After my sister and I left home, she went to work for the U.S. State Department and lived and traveled all over the world. She accumulated art, furniture, and whatever struck her fancy from many places, with a special emphasis on India and Vietnam. She has an eclectic sense of style and has combined her foreign treasures with heirlooms from my grandmother's family for a unique look.

If inherited furniture, artwork, or other heirloom pieces don't go with your decor, here are a few ideas:

- *Intermingle them with your own things, or add a few tie-in pieces to create an ageless, eclectic look.*
- *Collections or items with a similar theme will look best grouped together.*
- *If your heirloom linens are tucked away in the cupboard, take them out and use them every day.*
- *If your heirloom linens are too fragile to use, try hanging them in much the same way as tapestries.*
- *Frame lace or other small items in shadow boxes.*

If you don't have heirlooms or keepsakes in your family, or if you want new or different ones, you can create this tradition yourself. After all, heirlooms are created with each generation. Remember:

- *A keepsake is certainly a <u>treasure</u>, and it's usually something that reminds us of the person who owned it, but it can be something quite ordinary—such as a favorite pincushion; a collection of buttons, seashells, or silver spoons; a small lacquered box found in Chinatown; letters and foreign coins kept in a memory box; inexpensive jewelry such as club pins from high school or a childhood charm or ID bracelet.*

- *Heirlooms are more costly and rare, and may have significant personal meaning to the owner. Such heirlooms might be antique furniture, clothing and accessories, vintage bed linens, lace-trimmed handkerchiefs, hand towels or bureau scarves, good jewelry, china, a silver tea service or serving pieces, crystal and cut glass, pottery, and so forth. However, what you create yourself becomes an heirloom with the simple act of handing it down to your daughter.*

PART TWO

Celebrations and Holidays

Chapter 4

Weddings

Weddings embody tradition in almost every detail. They also engage us in a full range of emotions. Whether we smile during the best man's toast or get misty-eyed as the bride tucks her grandmother's lace handkerchief inside her sleeve, we realize that weddings can bring out different feelings in each of us. In fact, wedding traditions can be just as diverse as our emotions—circumspect, religious, symbolic, or lighthearted and fun.

Perhaps one reason we love weddings so much is that they're a very public celebration of love and commitment. Not only do a man and woman promise to love and cherish each other, they join together their past and future into the present. Weddings truly are the hallmark of new beginnings.

Theme and Celebrity Weddings

For most little girls, their first romantic fantasy is a lot like the fairy tale of Cinderella. She arrives at the ball in a coach drawn by four white horses, wears delicate glass slippers, and is "saved" from an ordinary life by a handsome and gallant young prince. Of course, for some of us, it was a fantasy that took flight when we watched young Lady Diana Spencer waving from the exquisite horse-drawn carriage that transported her from life as a kindergarten teacher to life as the Princess of Wales.

Theme weddings are a perfect way for mothers and daughters to re-create together the fairy-tale aura of youth. When planning her wedding last year, Billi went one step further and transformed her dream of a Cinderella wedding into reality. She used ice blue and silver as a color scheme, wore a dress with a fitted bodice and a ball gown skirt, and wore clear plastic slippers to simulate Cinderella's glass version.

The reception was held from eight in the evening till midnight—so the bride and groom could leave before her gown turned into rags! Place cards were not used at the reception. Instead, each table was named for a character or a place in the story. Guests received a card telling them at which table—King Stefan, the Palace, Cinderella, Gus, Jaq, or the Prince, for example—they were to be seated. Papier-mâché pumpkins decorated with opalescent paint and covered with sparkles were used for table centerpieces, guests received chocolate "glass" slippers as favors, and the newly married couple's first dance was "So This Is Love" from the movie's sound track. Although the wedding may have seemed like a fantasy, Billi says her "ultimate reason for having a Cinderella wedding is because my fiancé is a perfect prince, and I'm the lucky princess that found him."

Most mothers dream of the day their daughters announce their intention to marry (even if the prospective groom isn't a prince!). In our culture, the bride's family traditionally plans and pays for most of the wedding. Some brides and their mothers prefer small, intimate weddings, while others have large, grand affairs. Regardless of what size wedding they'd like to plan, a great way to get ideas is to look at trends in celebrity weddings. For instance, if you want a lavish wedding, take some tips from comedienne Joan Rivers, whose daughter, Melissa, got married a few years ago. Rivers spent close to $1 million to turn the New York Plaza Hotel into a fantasy winter extravaganza, and in an entrance equal to any entrance in any Broadway show, Joan entered the elegant reception ballroom to the tune of "Hey, Big Spender." Melissa added a sentimental touch by honoring both her mother's heritage and memories of her father with a Russian theme that included several miniature Fabergé eggs crafted in the 1800s that her father had given her.

Some celebrity women are just like the girl next door and choose smaller, more intimate weddings. If keeping things low-key is at the top of your list, take into consideration how super-model Cindy Crawford planned her wedding on Paradise Island in the Bahamas. Although she kept things sweet and simple, she also wanted part of her heritage included in the celebration. As a tribute to her grandmother and as a symbol of lasting tradition, she had replicas made of the pipe cleaner bride and groom that topped her grandmother's wedding cake over sixty years ago.

The Rings

British actress Kate Winslet chose a traditional place for her wedding—the chapel near her family's home in England where she'd been baptized. Kate and her fiancé also decided on traditional white-gold wedding bands, a personification of everlasting love and commitment. Without a doubt, the most sentimental piece of jewelry throughout the world is the wedding ring. The first wedding rings were made of rushes, braided grass, leather, bone, or ivory, and were later created from iron, silver, and gold. Rings continue to be the most recognizable symbol of marriage throughout most of the world.

If you're fortunate enough to receive an heirloom engagement ring or wedding band from your mother, future mother-in-law, or grandmother, you've become a link in a special chain of tradition. My mother has jewelry she's collected from all over the world, and she's been passing pieces on to my sister, me, and my daughter for some time now. When my son, Brian, became engaged, she gave him a large square-cut aquamarine and six small diamonds to have made into an engagement ring for his fiancée. It was a very special way to welcome Brian's future wife, Gia, into the family.

Cultural Traditions

Around the world, cultures and ethnic groups celebrate weddings with their own unique customs. The French have a lovely tradition of giving the bridal toast with a special two-handled cup called the *coupe de marriage,* which is passed down through families for generations. Germans tend to celebrate weddings over several days, and the Greeks "crown" the bride and groom to show that the couple are the king and queen of their union. The Amish traditionally marry on a weekday after the harvest season so everyone in the community can attend, and Quaker brides present themselves to the groom, rather than being "given away," because a Quaker woman knows that she belongs to no one but herself.

In Great Britain during Victorian times, a bride placed sixpence in her shoe to bring the couple wealth in their married life. Some brides still place a shiny penny in their shoe, and if the bride if especially lucky, the coin will have special meaning. My friend Barbara had a lucky gold piece that belonged to her grandmother. She gave it to her daughter, Katie, to wear in her shoe on her wedding day, and plans to continue the tradition when her other daughter, Kelly, marries.

If your family doesn't have a special coin, buy one or two with personal significance from a coin dealer. Choose coins minted the year you and your fiancé were born, the year your parents married, or a coin from the country of your ancestors.

In Mexico, the groom presents his bride with thirteen gold coins as his promise to support her. The coins are presented in a small chest, or *arras,* which symbolizes wealth and strength. Jewish tradition also encompasses this public expression of a husband's ability to care for and support his wife. A document called a *ketubah* is drawn up before the marriage and records the financial obligations the husband undertakes on behalf of his wife. The *ketubah* protects the bride both within the marriage and in case of divorce, and also holds deep religious significance.

Another Jewish tradition is called the *krenzel* (crowning). When a woman's last daughter is wed, the mother is seated in the center of the room during the reception and crowned with a wreath of flowers. Then all the daughters dance around her to a very lively song in celebration of their mother. Many cultures celebrate with traditional dances at wedding receptions. The Irish have the *janting char,* during which the groom is presented to the guests while being carried in a chair, and Jewish custom embraces the *hora,* a traditional dance of celebration.

Kim, a sales director for an Internet company, was born in Hawaii. When she planned her wedding reception, she decided to follow the Hawaiian tradition of dancing a hula for her husband, Tom. Kim performed the dance to a song about the *maile lei* while wearing her flowing satin wedding gown. Through graceful movements of her hands and arms, Kim expressed her love for her husband, something Tom says he'll remember for the rest of his life.

If your wedding, or that of your daughter, is still a gleam in your eye, you have plenty of time to research the wedding traditions and customs of your ancestors. Not only would it be an interesting project, but you might be able to incorporate or adapt some of those old customs into a modern wedding.

- *Ask your mother and grandmother to tell you about their weddings and those of their parents. Be sure and tell them you want to learn about traditions having to do with family, ancestry, and religion.*
- *Once you've got a starting point on ancestry or religion, you can use the Internet to research further. Choose any search engine, combine your ancestry with the phrase "wedding traditions," and investigate the web sites that will come up.*
- *An excellent resource that covers a dozen religions and more than 125 countries is "Weddings, Dating, and Love Customs of Cultures Worldwide, Including Royalty," by Carolyn Mordecai.*

Wedding Attire

Many brides wear something handed down from their mothers as part of their wedding ensemble. This tradition was especially meaningful for Carolyn, an administrative assistant to a federal judge. She was thrilled when her daughter, Adele, wanted to wear her gown for her wedding: "It was cream satin, fitted in a princess style with an empire waist, and a lace bodice. It had been taken up to fit me (oh, those wonderful days when I weighed only ninety-eight pounds!). We took it to a tailor who let the seams out. When I took it to the cleaner's in preparation for the wedding, they said this type of material is not even made anymore. I am sure my mother was with me when I chose it and paid a princely sum (in those days) of $110." Adele also used one of the songs from her mother's wedding, "Jesu, Joy of Man's Desiring." That song, and the gown, now have a doubly beautiful meaning for both mother and daughter.

Michele will always remember the morning of her wedding. Just before she left the house, her mother gave her a handkerchief her own mother had worn as a baby bonnet. She also gave her a locket with pictures of Michele's grandmother and grandfather inside. Michelle carried the handkerchief with her bridal bouquet, and after the wedding she placed both the handkerchief and the locket in a glass display case as a memento.

Garters are another traditional wedding memento. Mellissa, who works with physically and mentally challenged adults, found her mother's garter packed away in a box in the basement. "It was somewhat faded and the little silk flower was crushed," she says, "but it was then that I thought I'd like to wear it and start a new family tradition. We're going to replace the flower and the satin bow, and I'm going to embroider Mom's initials on it, and add mine after the wedding." There's room on the other side of the bow for more initials, and Mellissa hopes she'll have a daughter one day to carry the tradition into a third generation.

What if your mother didn't have a beautiful wedding gown or

her veil hasn't survived the years very well? You can still bridge the generations by including a part of Mom's wedding on your own special day. Karen made a "remembrance table" for her wedding reception. She created a traditional motif by draping her mother's antique lace veil around a group of old family photographs, which hid the damaged part of the veil.

Consider framing your mother's wedding invitation in an antique silver frame and adding whatever memorabilia she saved—delicate, faded roses from her wedding corsage, your father's boutonniere, the family prayer book, a Bible, or a rosary.

Flowers and the Bouquet

Of all the flourishes, settings, and special touches that mark a wedding, flowers are one of the most memorable. Flowers take on a special meaning in weddings, whether they take the form of a simple hand-tied spray of orange blossoms or the trailing bouquet of roses, lily of the valley, and gardenias that Sara Ferguson, soon to become the Duchess of York, chose when she married Great Britain's Prince Andrew. Flowers are highly charged symbols for a bride, setting the stage for both the wedding and the reception. Fresh flowers can even make a spectacular topper for a wedding cake.

Even if you aren't engaged, plan ahead! Ask the women who are important to you (sisters, daughters, mother, nieces, aunts, and friends) to save petals from their bouquets. Dry these petals and save them for your flower girl to strew down the aisle, or make sachets as remembrances for bridesmaids. If you're heading down the aisle soon, you can recall the romance of your courtship by having rose petals from the bouquet he gave you on your first date strewn down the aisle as you make your entrance. A friend of mine recently read about a wedding held on the bride's parents' twenty-fifth anniversary. Her mother had saved her wedding bouquet all those years, and she and her husband showered the bride and groom with flower petals that symbolized their many years of happiness.

Here are more innovative ideas for using flowers:

- *Bundle rose petals in circles of tulle tied with ribbon as favors for guests.*
- *Pass around a basket filled with rose petals and ask your guests to throw them instead of rice when you leave the church.*

Wedding Albums

Heather, a recent bride, was thrilled when her mother gave her the wedding album she'd started when she married. The wedding had been small, so only a few pages had been filled in. Heather's mom asked if she wanted to combine the old with the new by continuing the album with her own wedding memories to create a new tradition—an heirloom mother/daughter album filled with history, sentiment, and memories from both weddings.

A personalized wedding album, rather than a formal one, is a particularly special heirloom to share with your children and grandchildren. Megan, a newlywed in her twenties, suggests having guests sign the first few pages of a blank journal, then filling the rest of the book with special memories of the day. You could even add photos of the wedding and the honeymoon.

Another way to make your wedding album a true heirloom piece is to make copies of mementos from your mother's and grandmother's weddings. A few examples would be invitations, newspaper announcements, photographs, or pressed flowers from their bouquets. Ask what music was played at their weddings or which poems or prayers were offered. Write the words on a piece of parchment paper, or get a copy of the music's score, and add to the album as special remembrances.

The mother of the bride can also send blank album pages to the invited guests about a month before the wedding. Everyone could write remembrances about the couple, write a poem, copy a love sonnet out of a book, or paste photos of the bride or groom on the blank pages. The completed album should be presented to the couple on their wedding day.

The Dowry and Trousseau

The concept of a *dowry* goes back hundreds of years to when a bride's value was expressed in the value of her *trousseau,* or the property she brought into the marriage, including personal clothing, household linens, and bedding. This tradition spans many cultures, but in America it started in rural communities, then spread to cities everywhere. The trousseau is a compelling tradition that affirms the importance of the home and new life of the bride.

Shopping for a trousseau today can be especially memorable when a mother organizes the shopping excursions, helping her daughter decide what to buy or perhaps even what to make by hand. Although most brides receive household items as gifts, it's still a good idea to acquire the basic necessities for your new home or even your wardrobe. Here are a few suggestions for a modern trousseau:

- *Bedroom attire, including nightgowns, peignoirs, teddies, a robe, slippers, and pretty lingerie, as well as candles, scents, and oils.*
- *Clothing and accessories for work, home, play, and sports or outdoor activities.*
- *Bed linens, including sheets, pillows, comforters, and quilts.*
- *Formal tablecloth, napkins, and table runner in fine linen or lace.*
- *An adequate supply of linens for the kitchen, including towels, everyday placemats, cloth napkins, and items such as a tea cozy, toaster cover, and so forth.*

- *Bath linens, towels and accessories, scented soaps, lotions, and floating candles.*

Hope Chests

After the American Revolution, the tradition of the *hope chest* started because many brides' personal items were stored in large wooden chests. Although the American version of the hope chest was a well-made, handcrafted family heirloom using hardwood such as oak or cherry, a young woman could cover a heavy box or inexpensive pressed sawdust chest with upholstery material or heavy tapestry fabric for a unique look. In today's busy world, you might be more likely to buy items for your hope chest than to make them, but this old tradition is being resurrected by modern mothers and daughters during their "waiting game."

Nancy's mother taught her to sew, both by hand and by machine, when she was a girl, and together they made household items for Nancy's hope chest—tablecloths, pillowcases, hand towels, placemats, and samplers. By the time she turned twenty-five, Nancy had a huge, beautiful hope chest full of things but no "knight in shining armor," so she started calling the box her "hopeless chest."

"Suddenly, I gave everything to my mother and my brother's wives. They reluctantly accepted these treasures of mine, and when I met my husband-to-be shortly thereafter, everyone offered things back. I refused because I loved walking into their homes and seeing the things that I had made with such hope displayed with love. My mother kept many of the things, and when she passed away, they came back to me. Now, when my daughter, Liz, and I sew together, I hear myself reminding her to make tiny stitches and try to have her work as neat on the back as on the front. I hear myself saying, 'Nana always told me that if . . .' "

If you have a hope chest, when Mr. Right does come along all the treasures will be brought out and used in your home. At the same time, pack the memories and keepsakes from your wedding inside, along with a letter to the daughter you hope to have one day.

Mother/Daughter Traditions

Just as marriage joins the lives of two people into one, it can also move the mother/daughter relationship into a new realm of understanding, acceptance, and love. Weddings are beginnings, hopes for the future, and full of promise. There are several ways to take the time to make this special day a pivotal moment in your mother/daughter relationship.

Although bridesmaids traditionally dress the bride for her wedding, you can still find a way to share this intimate moment with your mother. Ask her to help you with your veil or with buttoning all those tiny pearl buttons. The *real* tradition is the importance of spending time with her before the ceremony. You could also include her in the ceremony itself by having both your mother *and* your father walk down the aisle with you. You might also consider asking her to be your matron of honor.

"Something old, something new, something borrowed, something blue" is a familiar wedding tradition that weaves generations together in the hearts and minds of women everywhere. Some traditions happen by chance, others because women's thoughts naturally turn to the need to remember and to celebrate these special moments with those yet to follow. If there's *one* day every woman remembers, it's the day she marries. If there's a second day, it's the day her *daughter* marries.

Here are a few thoughts on wedding traditions, whether you're starting new ones, embellishing the tried and true, or just sharing ideas:

- *Write a letter to your mother (or daughter) telling her how much she means to you and how she's changed your life. Think back to moments in your life when you felt especially close, when she listened to your problems, encouraged you, or helped you. Put your feelings into handwritten words, and give her the letter before the ceremony.*

- *Have an intimate lunch with your mother (or daughter) a few days before the wedding. Share an hour or two, talking and reflecting on the past and planning for the future.*
- *If your mother is lost to you, look among your family and friends for a woman who could act as a friend, companion, and guide. If you see a daughter who needs a mothering hand, offer yours.*
- *Instead of having wedding guests sign a book, find a beautiful mat at a framing shop, mount your invitation on one side and a sheet of handmade paper on the other for guests to sign. After the wedding, frame the mat and hang it in your new home.*

Chapter 5

Holidays

When we think of holidays, we think of family get-togethers, favorite foods, laughter, and celebration. Whether it's a cultural holiday like St. Patrick's Day, a national commemoration such as Independence Day, or a religious observance like Christmas or Hanukkah, a holiday is also a time of good cheer, thanks, and reflection. The sights, sounds, and smells of holidays take us back in time to childhood and to the warmth and love of women who are the heart of family traditions. The best holiday celebration anyone can have is to be with family—making, sharing, and keeping traditions.

July Fourth

Independence Day is one of my favorite holidays. Summer is such a great time to gather with family and friends to honor and celebrate our country's freedom. When my sister and I were small, we visited my grandparents every summer in a small town in Missouri, just a few miles from where I was born. The backyard had a vegetable garden and apple trees. We used to pick the best apples so my grandmother could make apple pie. On July Fourth, we ate pie still warm from the oven with a scoop of vanilla ice cream on top, while my grandfather set up fireworks. We always pestered him to let us light the fuses, but of course he never would. So we settled for sparklers, which reminded me of the bright fireflies that we caught in mason jars when dusk fell. On hot evenings my

Old-Fashioned Lemonade

12 to 15 fresh lemons
2 cups water
1 cup sugar
Fresh mint leaves

Cut the lemons in half, extract the juice, and drain to remove the seeds and pulp. Set aside. In a 3-quart saucepan, combine the water and sugar and bring to a boil. Reduce the heat and stir for a minute or two until the sugar dissolves. Let cool and pour into a 2-quart pitcher. Add the lemon juice and stir. Refrigerate, and serve over ice cubes. Garnish with mint leaves.

grandmother also made old-fashioned lemonade that we seemed to drink by the gallon.

Memories of the Fourth of July stayed with me after my children were born. When they were small and fireworks were still legal in California, we put on our own fireworks display. At least a dozen neighborhood kids joined us, and I always served old-fashioned lemonade, just like my grandmother. I always bought my favorite fireworks from childhood, too—rockets and fountains that filled the sky with silver and red showers, gold flowers that turned to blue, and colored comet tails that spun in circles. I always passed around dozens of small boxes of sparklers and magic snakes to all the kids, and I remember that my daughter especially liked to twirl around with a sparkler in one hand, writing her name in the air.

Val's family celebrates the Fourth of July in much the same way every year, with a group of relatives and friends who have known each other for most of their lives, including three groups of mothers and daughters. "We all meet at one family's beach home that overlooks the San Juan Islands on Puget Sound in Washington State." "We all bring our favorite foods—the ones we're 'known' for. Joy brings potato salad, barbecued chicken, and baked beans; her daughter, Gayle, makes a cheesecake we dream about all year; Felicia finds the freshest corn on the cob; Olive brings apple pie 'to die for'; and Karla makes a mean 'cowboy casserole.' I help with the ribs, and my daughter, Amy, and daughter-in-law, Kristine, make a wonderful fruit platter. Late in the evening, we cook fresh crabs and oysters in crab pots right on the beach, and gather the children around the fire to make 'smores' and watch fireworks.

"Although we all enjoy the feast, the best part of the day is reconnecting with everyone and getting to see all our lovely daughters, how they've grown up, and what they're doing with their lives. Every year, we moms talk about our own mothers and the times when they used to spend the day with us. As we gather together, we know their memories will live on in their daughters and granddaughters."

Don't forget, too, that July Fourth is an important national holiday. It's a good time to teach your daughter about the Revolutionary War, the Declaration of Independence, and Betsy Ross. You can also tour the White House by accessing the Internet at www.whitehouse.gov/WH/kids/html/home.html, where you'll find a child's eye view of the history of the presidency and the White House, as well as personal information about past presidents, their families, and their pets.

The Holiday Season

When the reds and golds of autumn fade and the days get perceptibly shorter, the holiday season is just around the corner. Starting with the bounty of Thanksgiving and Kwanzaa, and continuing through the festivities of Christmas, Hanukkah, and New Year, magic will soon fill the air. Traditions are a focal point of the holiday season, and many of those traditions include beloved dishes prepared the same way and served year after year. Whether you serve turkey or prime rib as a main course, it's not only the taste of food but its presentation and setting that make people slow down and take notice. If you have your mother's silver, or your grandmother's china, this is the time of year to set a beautiful holiday table. Combining the old with the new brings back memories of years gone by and strengthens the traditions of today.

Autumn's Bounty

Thanksgiving and Kwanzaa are times when we give thanks for the fruits and bounty of the harvest (although Kwanzaa is celebrated in late December). This is also a time to recommit ourselves to a better life for our communities, families, and those we love. The quiet, early morning hours are spent preparing a meal that celebrates a family's hard work, good fortune, and hospitality. In most families, it's considered an honored rite of passage to be the one to prepare and host these most festive celebrations of the family.

In years gone by, women would start cooking the day before the feast. Today, it's much the same for Lyn, a family nurse practitioner. For the past twenty years, the women in her family, and a few friends, have gotten together for a "pre-Thanksgiving" cook fest. Although this is the time they dice the celery and onions for the dressing and put together anything else they need to do, Lyn confides that the primary reason they get together is to talk: "We have some wine, put on some real tearjerker music, and happily dice celery and onions. Whoever needs a good cry the most gets to do the onions, and it usually takes us a good three hours or so to do the preparations *properly.* By properly, I mean we must talk about the previous year, what has happened this year, and how thankful we are for what we have. We then proceed to solve the problems of the world—poverty, domestic violence, war, and drugs—as well as recall memories of those who have passed on. Then it is time for the Scrabble tournament.

"As my Grannie aged, she did less of the chopping but stayed with us as far as the talking and stories. She would tell us tales of hoboes coming to her home, and say that she never turned anyone away for a meal. She used to say, 'You never know, it may be Jesus coming to your door.' We didn't know until a couple of years ago that there were 'hobo' signs on her fence that distinguished her home from the others as a place where you could get a meal. We don't have Grannie anymore, but we have my mom, sister, friends, and now my six-year-old niece to join in. My niece is too young to chop, but she will still be with us in the kitchen doing the 'girl' thing. It is a tradition that grounds us and binds us—woman to woman."

As most of us know, food isn't just about feeding people, it's about relationships. The women in Lyn's family are participating in a ritual that honors and celebrates the bonds between them. By inviting Lyn's six-year-old niece to join them, they are also giving her entrance into their circle of friendship.

After Thanksgiving dinner, Becka's family traditionally spent the evening putting up their Christmas tree. Although November 25 might seem a bit early to some, her family enjoyed having an entire month to celebrate. They decorated the tree with ornaments that had been passed down through the years or handmade by the children in the family. Becka also remembers the scents of the season—bayberry candles, potpourri, and fresh evergreen garlands. "After the tree was up we would turn off the lights and sit and look at our beautiful creation, marvel at its beauty, and eat the pumpkin pie we had been smelling all day." The holidays are still so very special to me. Mom, me, and my two daughters all live together now, so I get to spend holidays with the mother who gave me a tradition I hope to carry out for generations. For me, Thanksgiving is a time to reflect on all those wonderful years."

You can pass traditions down from mother to daughter, you can build on them, or you can be the magician who waves her magic wand and creates new ones. Holiday traditions are everywhere around you. Just pick the ones you want and make them happen.

Mother/Daughter Moments

A special Christmas remembrance for Adrienne takes her back to Chicago and can easily be duplicated wherever you live. When she was a little girl growing up in Chicago, each year her mother took her downtown to Marshall Field's to have lunch in the Walnut Room. "We would also spend quite a bit of time walking down

State Street looking at the animated decorated windows. We left Chicago when my daughter was four, but returned many years later after Ashley was born. For three years, until we all moved to Arizona, we did the Marshall Field's lunch event by the Christmas tree."

Choose a favorite restaurant with wonderful holiday decorations for a special mother/daughter lunch of your own, no matter what your age. It's a good idea to plan this outing for early December to avoid some of the crowds.

Gift Wrapping

Adrienne has another Christmas custom you can easily bring into your own holiday traditions. Adrienne's aunt was a fashion designer who exuded creativity and style. Her presents were one-of-a-kind fantasies, wrapped with beautiful paper, delicate laces, and ribbons in every color. "Every year, I looked forward to seeing how she wrapped the gifts almost as much as the gifts themselves. Although I envied her talent, when my children were young it was all I could do to put paper on a gift and a self-stick bow and a name tag. After the children were on their own, though, I started decorating the packages with the same flourish my aunt displayed. Each present was uniquely wrapped, complete with embellishments and beautiful handmade bows and name tags. I probably spend a half hour wrapping each gift. I love the way they look under the tree, and it's great fun to watch everyone inspect the gifts to see which ones are theirs."

Adrienne's daughter decided to follow her example because she wants her Christmas to be "just like Mom's." Now it's a family joke that every night from the beginning of December until Christmas Eve, Adrienne and Jackie stay up until all hours wrapping presents, although Adrienne does admit the last-minute gifts usually get a stick-on bow and store-bought gift tag.

Here are a few ideas for one-of-a-kind gift wrappings:

- *Decide on a color scheme. Use either a few colors and patterns that work well together, or an array of colors, patterns, and textures. If you're not familiar with an artist's "color wheel," you can find one in art supply stores. Choose colors that lie next to each other on the color wheel and have similar values, like blue and green or red and gold, or colors that lie opposite each other, like red and green. Another idea is to use varying shades of two colors—and, of course, the standard Christmas colors of red, green, gold, and silver always work well, either in patterns, in solid colors, or in any combination of the two.*
- *Find a wholesale floral supply or craft store that carries special ribbons in all colors, sizes, and patterns. Experiment with the kind of wide ribbons made of sheer fabric that have thin wire embedded on both edges. Also check fabric stores for lace; unusual trims; and grosgrain, velvet, and satin ribbons.*
- *The fabric store is also a gold mine for alternatives to wrapping paper—buy lengths of velvet, gold and silver lamé, cotton with holiday themes, delicate laces, or tulle netting to wrap over colored paper.*
- *Cut patterns out of sponges in the shape of a leaf, star, snowman, or other holiday motif, dip in paint, and press on plain paper. You can also buy rubber stamps in holiday designs and stamp pads in a variety of colors.*
- *Have your children draw designs with crayons, colored pens, or pastels on white butcher paper to use for family gifts.*

Christmas Tree Snow

⅔ cup liquid starch
2 cups Ivory soap flakes
2–4 tablespoons water
Blue food coloring

Mix the liquid starch and Ivory flakes together in a bowl. Add the water and beat with a mixer until the solution thickens and becomes stiff. Add the food coloring a drop at a time while mixing until the snow turns icy white. Paint on Christmas tree branches.

A White Christmas

Lori's family moved into a new house when she was five. She remembers that it snowed that year, and was so cold there were icicles hanging from the kitchen faucet. "I woke up in the morning and walked through the French doors leading into the living room. With all of the snow outside and the white walls, the room was glowing! I felt like I was waking up in my own little castle. The tree was beautiful and had old-fashioned lights—not the small ones you buy now. My sisters and I lay beneath the tree and looked up through the center at all the beautiful colors. I remember the smell of the cedar logs burning in the stove and what the tree and the house looked like and even what my sisters and parents looked like, but for the life of me, I can't remember what presents I opened."

If you want to create your own white Christmas, start with homemade snow for the Christmas tree (at left).

The True Meaning of Christmas

What *is* the true meaning of Christmas? It shouldn't be nonstop shopping, charging too much on your credit cards, worrying that Uncle Joe won't like his gift, and being afraid that Aunt Jane will return whatever you buy her. Christmas should be about family, love, peace, and harmony, but it's all too easy to get caught up in the commercial whirlwind of the holiday season.

Jeannette is a full-time mom and has also adopted several

Christmas traditions that focus on family and faith rather than gifts. "To help our children focus on the real meaning of Christmas, we decided to limit our gifts to three per child each year. These gifts are representative of the three gifts to the Christ Child. First is the gift of gold. This is always an ornament that signifies some special memory, accomplishment, or interest of the previous year. This year, my daughter, Abigail, danced the part of an angel in our city ballet's production of *The Nutcracker,* so her ornament was a gold angel with a Nutcracker charm on a ribbon wrapped around the angel. Another benefit of the gift of gold is that the children will have their own very special collection of ornaments to take with them when they leave our home. Abigail really looks forward to unpacking all her special ornaments each year and hanging them on the tree while recalling the significance of each ornament. The next gift represents frankincense, a spice used in worship. Abigail learned to read this year, so we gave her a leather-covered large-print Bible to make it easier for her to follow along in Sunday school. The third gift represents myrrh, a rare and costly perfume. This is the extravagant, heart's desire gift, not so much what a child might need but what he or she really wants."

Christmas Story Basket

Another tradition Jeannette's family celebrates is the Christmas story basket: "Each year I collect Christmas storybooks, some old and some new. On the last night of November I stay up and wrap the books collected that year, along with old favorites collected and read in previous years. I wrap each one in red, green, or white tissue paper, put them all in a big basket tied with a festive bow, and place the basket near our reading corner. Each evening in December, the children take turns unwrapping a book to be read aloud before bed. My daughter has old book friends that she eagerly looks forward to seeing again each year—*A Bird's Christmas Carol,* by Kate Douglas Wiggin, and *Lion in the Box,* by Marguerite de Angeli. Often, after her younger brothers have been safely tucked in, Abigail will creep out of her room for a private read-aloud with me of the book that did not get finished that evening. These quiet, shared moments will always be precious to me."

Christmas Eve Box

A third tradition Jeannette's family has adopted is the Christmas Eve box: "We start with a light supper of some favorite food served in front of the fireplace by the tree. My daughter loves helping with this part. Then we bring out the hot chocolate, a plate of Christmas cookies, and the Christmas Eve box while carols play in the background. The box contains the same individually wrapped items each year. On top is a pair of new socks for each member of the family, then a new pair of pajamas. Last year I made Abigail a white flannel gown with a matching one for her doll. Both she and her doll have worn those to many slumber parties.

"At the bottom of the box is a new game, which we play together while comfily attired in our new pj's. My daughter is eight, loves these traditions, and looks forward to each one. They are like familiar pegs where she knows she can hang her special things. My hope is that she will one day pass these traditions (as well as some new ones of her own) along to her own family."

The Christmas Eve box and the Christmas story basket can easily become traditions in any family. These traditions do take some time and preparation, but they are also inexpensive ways to make the holiday season brighter. When you think back, you'll discover that these are the key ingredients to the real meaning of the holiday season. When you keep that uppermost in your holiday planning, you'll also find you've unwrapped the best present of all—spending time together.

Christmas Tree

It is thought that the Christmas tree is borrowed from early medieval religious plays performed in churches and town squares in Europe during the Advent season. The plays told the story of life from Adam and Eve in the Garden of Eden till the birth of Jesus in Bethlehem. A great tree was placed on the stage and hung with apples to symbolize the Garden of Eden, and people soon adopted the custom of putting a "paradise tree" in their homes at Christmas. The trees would be laden with gifts and lit with candles to celebrate paradise regained through the coming of Christ.

When I was growing up, we bought our Christmas tree at a lot in town. Of course, I knew the trees grew in the forest, and I had a vague understanding that someone had chopped down all those trees and brought them into town, but that's as much as I thought about it. When my children were quite young, we moved from Arizona to northern California and started some new holiday traditions. Our favorite was cutting down our own Christmas tree and bringing it home. When you go to the tree farm, you get a saw, you pick the tree you want, you cut it down, and then you tie it on top of your car or put it in the trunk of your car. I was a single mom at the time and knew there was no way I was getting a tree on top of my car, so I'd thought ahead and brought a cord to tie the trunk closed.

The kids and I spent a couple of hours finding the *perfect* tree, chopping it down, and hauling it to the car. That's when I realized how much bigger a tree is when it's lying on the ground than when it's growing in the forest. The tree was huge. I chopped another foot off the bottom of the tree and somehow got it into the trunk. Then we shared a

Christmas Tree Stars

Cut out two matching stars and decorate with colored markers, glitter, paint, stickers, crayons, colored pencils, beads, or sequins. Glue the pieces together back-to-back, leaving the bottom open so the star can be slipped on top of the tree. If you have more than two children, make more stars!

Ribbon or Paper Chains

Cut leftover or recycled ribbons (or strips of red and green construction paper) into six-to-eight-inch strips. Glue the ends of one strip together, then run another piece of ribbon or paper through this link and glue the ends, making a long chain as you go along.

Popcorn-and-Cranberry Garland

Pop plain corn (no salt or butter), and dry fresh cranberries on a paper towel. Thread a sewing needle with heavy-duty thread and "sew" the popcorn and cranberries together into a long chain.

picnic lunch, a thermos of hot cocoa, and anticipation of the holidays. When we got home, we lugged the tree into the house and discovered it was still too tall! This time, I cut some off the top of the tree, which didn't do much for its shape, but it was still our *perfect* tree. The next year we were better at choosing the tree, but we never had more fun than the year we established this family tradition. As you might imagine, my children tell and retell this story every year, and every year the tree grows taller with the telling.

Deborah, a mathematician, has done away with the elaborate ornament for the top of her family's Christmas tree. Instead, her daughter and son make a new star every year as a tree topper (see box on page 69). This is a fun project for young children, and easy, too.

There are many holiday craft projects you can enjoy with your children. Old-fashioned garlands, star tree toppers, Christmas cards, and holiday ornaments are just a few. At the left are two types of garlands to wrap around the tree, along a fireplace mantel, or on a staircase for an old-fashioned Christmas look.

Christmas Cards

Another familiar holiday tradition is Christmas cards. They started in Victorian times and have continued unabated through today. Sir Henry Cole, who worked for the British postal service, is credited with making the first card when he hired an artist to depict a Christmas scene framed in three panels. The center featured a family raising their glasses for a toast, and depicted on side panels were acts of charity—feeding the hungry and clothing the poor.

There are many ways to recycle Christmas cards. My favorite is to use them as package tags for next year's gifts. Just cut out what you think would make a pretty tag, punch a hole in the top with a paper punch, and use a ribbon to attach to the gift. Sometimes you can even get multiple tags from one card or use the whole front of the card as a tag for larger gifts.

Holiday Baking

No holiday is complete without the tradition of baking. Sugar cookies, plum pudding, fruitcake, cranberry bread, and many more festive sweets are a Christmas tradition in many families. Adrienne sets aside an entire day, and her daughter, daughter-in-law, and granddaughters all come to her house to bake. They make snowballs, sugar cutout cookies, candy cane sugar cookies, and pecan crescents.

Every culture has special dishes for its holidays. Deborah is Jewish, and she had her own childhood favorites: "Mum always made latkes (potato pancakes), and after I learned to make the traditional jelly doughnuts at school, it was my job to make them for the family. There were always special foods to enjoy during the holidays—matzoh ball soup for Passover, latkes and jelly

Snowball Cookies

2 sticks margarine or unsalted butter
½ cup powdered (confectioners') sugar
2 cups all-purpose white flour
1 teaspoon real vanilla
1 cup finely chopped pecans

Cream the margarine or butter and sugar together, then add the other ingredients. Mix well and form into balls approximately 2 inches in diameter. Place on an ungreased baking sheet and bake at 350° for 20 minutes. Let cool and roll in powdered sugar.

Potato Latkes

3 or 4 large potatoes, peeled
   and coarsely grated
1 small onion (optional),
   coarsely grated
2 eggs, beaten
2 to 3 tablespoons flour
1 to 1½ teaspoons salt, to taste
⅛ to ¼ teaspoon pepper, to
   taste
½ cup oil

Mix all the ingredients except the oil and let stand for 10 to 15 minutes to thicken. Heat the oil in a frying pan until small bubbles appear when you insert the tip of a wooden spoon. Then use a slotted spoon to place heaping tablespoons of the mixture into the pan. When the latkes are brown around the edges, turn over and fry until golden brown. Drain on paper towels and serve with applesauce or sour cream.

doughnuts for Hanukkah, honey cake for Rosh Hashanah, and cheesecake for Shavuot."

Hanukkah

Hanukkah, the Festival of Lights, is an eight-day Jewish holiday celebrating the liberation of Jerusalem. When the Hebrews were preparing to rededicate their temple, they found enough oil to light the temple lamp for only one day. According to legend, the oil lasted for eight days, and the lighting of candles (on the menorah, a nine-branch candelabrum) for eight consecutive nights has become the traditional way to celebrate Hanukkah. Children also receive presents or money during this celebration, which usually coincides with the Christmas season.

Ruth, a pediatrics nurse, celebrates each year with both Santa Claus and a menorah. "My husband and I feel that culture and education are important for our two daughters, regardless of religion. We don't identify ourselves as being either Jewish or Christian, and we talk openly about both faiths. I think it's healthy for Stephanie and Alyssa to know the differences, and for them to know people don't necessarily have all the answers to questions of faith. Kids of all religions can enjoy Santa Claus, as it has no basis in faith. We don't practice the American Jewish version of giving a present a day for Hanukkah, but adopted the European/Israeli version of giving Hanukkah money, so the kids can use it to buy holiday gifts."

The New Year

For Eastern countries, such as Japan and China, the holiday season centers on the New Year. Much like our Thanksgiving, this is a time to celebrate abundance, good health, and prosperity. New Year's celebrations in the Western world cap a long holiday season with parties, good company, and great food. Whether you're dancing till dawn and drinking champagne, watching fireworks in cities across America, or spending a quiet evening at home with family and friends, there's sure to be a toast to your good health and happiness in the coming year. Fill your holiday season with the following traditions that will bring meaning to your life and to the lives of others:

- *Christmas is a time for giving of ourselves. Donate money, make holiday baskets for the needy, serve dinner at a homeless shelter, or visit patients in a nursing home.*
- *Make it a tradition to invite someone who doesn't have family, or is far from home, to share your holiday dinner.*
- *If you always do the cooking on holidays, be sure to include your daughter, no matter her age, in planning the festivities, including choosing recipes, shopping, cooking, and entertaining. If your daughter is grown and lives nearby, ask her to host a get-together during the holidays that is all hers. It can be anything from a simple brunch before church or synagogue to a cocktail party or a sit-down dinner.*
- *Make a Christmas family scrapbook. Include copies of letters to Santa, photos of trimming the tree, favorite recipes, and family traditions such as attending church*

on Christmas Eve or searching for the perfect Christmas tree.

- *Make old-fashioned Christmas ornaments with your daughter from the many kits available. Choose from sequins and beads or fabric and trims that you glue or pin to Styrofoam shapes, ceramic ornaments that only need painting, or wood kits you glue together and paint.*

Chapter 6

Birthdays and Mother's Day

$\mathcal{M}$otherhood is a transforming event in many women's lives. When we celebrate a daughter's birthday, the hopes, fears, and priorities we have for her come into focus. Whether she's five, fifteen, or thirty, each year on this special day our thoughts return to the miracle of her birth and the day our life changed forever.

Our relationship with our own mother evolves through the years, too, especially when she becomes a grandmother. We tend to think it's the new mother who may not be ready for the transformation this baby daughter brings about. But what about the new grandmother? As her daughter becomes a mother, the role she has played for so many years changes yet again. These two important relationships—mother and daughter, daughter and mother—form a fluid, interconnected path throughout women's lives and beyond. We celebrate birthdays and Mother's Day to acknowledge the importance of these relationships and the impact they have on all that we do.

Birthday Parties and Little Girls

Deb has some wonderful birthday traditions, but this first one is my favorite. "One tradition that I really like takes place at bedtime on the night of Sarah's birthday. Bill and I tell her about the day she was born, what happened, how we felt, and all about that special day. Sarah really seems to like this quiet time together. We al-

Birthday Cookies

2 cups sugar
1 cup vegetable shortening
1 cup sour cream
3 eggs
½ teaspoon lemon extract
5 cups flour
1 teaspoon baking soda
½ teaspoon salt

Cream the sugar and vegetable shortening. Add the sour cream, eggs, and lemon extract. Mix well. Combine the dry ingredients and add together, mixing until well blended. Chill several hours. Roll the dough out on floured plastic wrap. Cut with floured cookie cutters. Bake at 375° for 7 to 8 minutes, until the edges begin to brown.

Icing

16 ounces sifted powdered
   (confectioners') sugar
3 or 4 tablespoons fresh-squeezed lemon
   juice

Combine the ingredients and beat until smooth. Separate into two bowls, add a few drops of food coloring in each, and stir. Decorate with sprinkles, colored sugars, tiny silver edible balls, chopped nuts, etc.

ways start with the words 'On the day you were born . . .' " (Adoptive parents can embrace this tradition, and make it even more poignant, by starting with "On the day you came into our hearts . . ." or "On the day we chose you to be part of our family . . .")

After Deb had her own children, she continued the tradition of having big birthday celebrations: "One year we arranged a treasure hunt, with bandanas and eye patches for all the kids, and a metal box we locked up with chains and hid behind the vegetable garden. The older kids were given maps with clues to lead them to the box, while younger children were given maps and clues to find the key that unlocked the box. At the end of the game, both groups converged on a treasure box filled with plastic jewelry, coins and compasses, and candy."

Cindy has always loved to cook. "My daughter is only six, but she already loves the kitchen. For her fifth birthday, she wanted a cookie-baking party and invited four of her best friends. I gave each guest a little apron with her name painted on it and a cookie cutter tied to the belt with ribbon. The girls had a great time making, decorating, and eating platefuls of birthday cookies."

This is a great way to have fun in the kitchen and show a handful of little girls how to cook one of their favorite foods.

When my children were growing up, we had two birthday traditions. The first was that I woke them up in the morning by singing a quick version of the "Happy Birthday" song, usually off-key. Everybody in my family has since adopted this tradition. We live some distance from one another, so the birthday person gets several phone calls on his or her special day, with voices singing "Happy Birthday"— and to keep the tradition the same, we *all* sing off-key! Our second tradition was a special birthday snowball cake. It's easy, tastes great, and looks even better.

> ### Snowball Cake
>
> 2-layer packaged devil's food
>   cake mix
> 6 ounces raspberry or
>   strawberry jam
> 16 ounces heavy cream,
>   whipped, or 16 ounces dairy
>   topping
> 4 ounces shredded coconut
>
> Prepare the cake mix according to the package directions, using two round cake pans. Spread jam on one layer of cake, then place the second layer on top. Ice with whipped cream or dairy topping. Sprinkle coconut on top and press around the sides of the frosted cake.

Tammy, a family educator for the Head Start program, decided to have a low-budget tea party for her daughter Jessi's eighth birthday. "For favors, we decorated inexpensive straw hats with silk flowers and ribbons I had in my craft supplies. The girls played 'makeup' and 'dress-up,' and my son served as the waiter for 'high tea.' We had peanut butter and jelly sandwiches (with the crusts removed), cream cheese and jelly sandwiches, chocolate-dipped strawberries, and cupcakes. I took a photo of the girls all dressed up and used copies of the photo for thank-you notes. For her ninth birthday, Jessi had a huge slumber party. Since her birthday is in the summer, we borrowed a large tent and put it in the

Birthday Stepping-stones

20- to 40-pound bag of
    premixed concrete
Water
Large plastic bucket
Shovel or large, sturdy stick to
    mix cement
Large foil roasting pan
Board for leveling cement
Petroleum jelly

Following the directions on the bag, mix enough cement and water in the bucket to fill the foil pan. Pour the cement into the foil pan and level the cement with the side of the board. Cover your daughter's hands or feet with petroleum jelly and press them into the cement. Add her signature or the date if you like. When the cement sets, turn the pan over and the block will pop out. Use as stepping stones in your yard.

front yard for all the festivities. First, we swam at the local pool, had hamburgers and cake, then had each girl make a tie-dye T-shirt big enough to sleep in. I took a photo of the girls in their shirts—it was dark already, but the photo came out really nice, so I made copies and slipped them in with the thank-you notes.

"As far as my personal feelings and memories regarding these birthday parties, I guess when we had the tea party it was something I would have loved having when I was a child. Jessi and I worked together to set it up and prepare the food. I felt a great sense of satisfaction that I could provide a special celebration for her, even when our budget was extremely tight. As for the slumber party, I did have one almost exactly the same when I turned ten. That's the only party I remember having with my friends, and we had so much fun I knew if I ever had children, at least one would have that kind of party. Jessi's party was the event of the neighborhood."

If you're looking for a unique way to memorialize your daughter's birthdays, you might try a variation on the handprints children make in kindergarten—birthday stepping-stones. If you don't have a yard big enough for stepping-stones, scale down by using less cement, a smaller foil pan, and filling the pan only half or a third full. You could use these smaller stones as personalized doorstops.

Celebrating Teenage Daughters

It's sometimes more difficult to plan birthday celebrations for teenage daughters because they may only want to do things with girlfriends. If your daughter prefers to celebrate with her friends, or only wants you to buy her something, here are a few ideas that might address this issue:

- *Most girls are interested in music and bands, and want to go to concerts. That's a great idea, as long as you tag along, even if you can't stand the music. Invite one of your girlfriends to go, too.*
- *Makeovers are popular with teenage girls, and available at beauty salons, cosmetology schools, or studio photographers who specialize in glamour shots. Invite your daughter's best friend to get a makeover, too, and tag along for the fun. Stroll along the mall afterward so they can show off their new looks.*
- *Slumber parties are popular into the teen years and a great way to have a low-cost celebration at home. Provide lots of snacks, but make a few yourself (such as cookies and homemade popcorn with toppings). That'll keep you in the kitchen and part of what's going on without seeming to eavesdrop. Rent a few movies—and buy yourself a pair of earplugs if you want to sleep.*

Adult Daughters

When daughters become adults, it's much easier to figure out what to do for their birthdays because you've probably become good friends. Invite them to do something you know they'd enjoy, whether that's cooking dinner and sharing a good bottle of wine, going to a play, attending a poetry reading, hiking in the hills, or going to a spa for the works. One year, my daughter surprised me with a visit to a salon for a facial and massage. It was something I would never have done for myself, and it made me feel like a pampered princess for a day.

Rose's family lives on a farm and raises sheep. Since any shepherd has a lot of wool, Rose dyes, spins, and knits for everyone in the family. Living in the country makes for a very different type of birthday celebration. "Every gathering is centered around a meal. As the girls have grown, I have less cooking to do when we have a party, and Heidi especially likes to cook. Two of my children were born in July, which is prime-time haying time. If we are getting the hay in from the fields on a birthday, the party won't be until all the hay is in, which is usually at dark. We always have the birthday girl's favorite meal, and she gets extra treats and lots of attention, so working on a birthday isn't so bad. Of course, the birthday girl doesn't have to do any of the dishes, no matter how many people are at the party. It's wonderful to gather like this, and even the kitchen work is fun when we're all doing it together."

Mother's Day

The earliest Mother's Day celebration can be traced to ancient Greece. In the springtime, the Greeks honored Rhea, the mother of the gods. During the 1600s, England commemorated a day called Mothering Sunday, when members of all social classes were encouraged to spend the day with their mothers. A special flourless cake, called the mothering cake, provided a festive touch for the occasion.

In 1872, Julia Ward Howe, who wrote the words to "The Battle Hymn of the Republic," suggested the idea of an American Mother's Day dedicated to peace. Ms. Howe began holding organized Mother's Day meetings, but it wasn't until 1907 that another woman, Ana Jarvis, began a campaign to establish a national Mother's Day. In 1914, President Woodrow Wilson officially established the second Sunday of May as Mother's Day, and today many other countries celebrate Mother's Day, even though they might do it at different times throughout the year.

When I was a little girl, my sister, Bonnie, and I made breakfast for our mom on Mother's Day. We fixed raisin toast, cereal, and orange juice, and always picked roses from the backyard to put in a bud vase for each place setting. My daughter, Heather, is four years older than her brother, so she usually commandeered him into helping put breakfast together for my special Mother's Day, too. Heather did something else special for two or three Mother's Days—she made up coupons, which she decorated, redeemable whenever I wanted. Although similar coupon books can now be found in stores, I much prefer the handmade variety. Here are a few I remember:

- *Being quiet so Mom can sleep until 10:00 A.M. on Saturday.*
- *Folding one basket of clean laundry and putting the clothes away.*
- *Vacuuming the living room.*
- *Extra hugs.*
- *Watering the garden.*

My grandmother was an invalid when I was a young girl, and I remember my mother buying her presents for Mother's Day—a bed jacket, an afghan, slippers, or nightgowns. Unfortunately, my grandmother never wore these gifts; she put them away because they were "too good" to use. That was frustrating for my mother, because we lived halfway across the country, and although we visited every year, she couldn't be with her mom on Mother's Day. Sometimes gifts aren't the answer for a variety of reasons, and sometimes we can't be with our mom or daughter either on her birthday or on Mother's Day.

If your mother lives a distance from you, or if she's passed away, why not visit a nursing home and brighten the day of a mother who might not have a daughter to make her feel special on *her* day? Melanie, a legal secretary, lost her mother a few years ago to cancer. "Losing Mom was hard. She'd battled cancer for five painful years, and I only got to spend a few weeks with her each year. I live in Virginia and have two daughters, six and nine, and Mom and Dad lived a thousand miles away. I really went into a depression around Mother's Day, and last year decided to do something about it. I called a nursing home and asked if I could visit with a mom who didn't have any family nearby. They gave me the names of two elderly women, and I decided to visit them both. I took small bouquets of flowers and spent about an hour with each of them. I also brought along photos of my mom and daughters. Next year, I'm going to take the girls along, too. They've lost their real grandma, but I found that there are a lot of grandmothers out there to go around."

The importance of celebrating birthdays, Mother's Day, or any tradition is to be with those you love. Here are a few thoughts to help you find something besides the usual flowers and fragrance:

- *Focus in on what your mother does in her spare time. What are her hobbies and avocations? Is there a way you can share them with her? If she gardens, attend a flower show; if she loves art, take her on a gallery crawl; if she loves to fish or hike, plan an outdoor excursion together.*

- *Encourage new interests—give the gift of a series of lessons in something she has expressed an interest in. Why not take lessons together?*

- *If your daughter has children, give her a Mother's Day off by taking her kids for the afternoon—or hire a baby sitter so you can do something together.*

Chapter 7

Everyday Celebrations

Do you remember a special day that just *seemed to happen*? It may have been a childhood afternoon you spent with your mother that made you feel special and particularly loved. Perhaps it was the time she took you for a walk, telling you the names of flowers you picked along the way and brought home to put in a jelly jar vase. Maybe it was the evening you spent talking to your daughter about school and boys, when you told her how you fell in love with her father. You might not have been doing anything special or planned; there are some times when an unexpected few hours become a memory that's *just right*. That's what I call an "everyday celebration," and although you can't repeat a perfect day, you *can* create more of them.

No matter your age or that of your daughter or mother, think of ways to break the regular routine. Everyday celebrations can be as simple as a picnic in the backyard or as elaborate as a weekend away from home.

Kimberleigh, an avid gardener, painter, and stay-at-home mom, has a perfect example of what I'm talking about: "On one of the first warm days of spring, my two preschoolers said, 'Mommy, come outside with us.' My hands were in the sink and the dryer buzzer had just gone off, and I thought about all the things I should be doing. Then I realized that I didn't have to do them right then. My girls each took one of my hands and pulled me out the door with anticipation shining on their faces. That's how we ended up in the middle of the street, in front of our house, flying kites on a weekday at two o'clock in the afternoon."

You don't have to be a stay-at-home mom to spend this special, unexpected time with daughters, but you do have to be aware of opportunities to carve time out of a busy schedule to experience the unexpected. When we're busy, we have a tendency to answer with an automatic no when daughters ask for something, even when it's something as important as time. We need to step back from our day-to-day routine and give our daughters that special one-on-one attention. Remember—you're creating memories, and you want them to be the kind your daughter will cherish.

Bedtime

Bedtime is a perfect opportunity to create warm, loving memories with your daughter. It's quiet, the day is done, and you have a few moments before she drifts off to dreamland. Rita, an attorney, finds bedtime to be her most favorite time of day. "I work long hours, so I make the most of the time I have with Stephanie and Jennifer. They're ten and eleven, and have separate rooms, so I have one-on-one time with each of them. Stephanie enjoys having me read aloud to her, but when I close the book, we talk about the story, the heroine, and what we think is going to happen next. After we say our prayers together, I go to tuck in Jennifer. She has ADD, and I've found that I need to do things a bit differently with her. First, I have her decide what she wants to wear the next day, and we set everything out. If she has too many decisions to make in the morning, she can get pretty distracted, and that makes for a stressful start of the day. Once she's settled in bed, I have Jennifer read to me. If I read to her, she tends to become impatient and her attention wanders too much.

"These quiet times with my daughters have become a tradition over the years. Each girl has my complete attention, if only for a half hour each evening. They've shared secrets, talked about somebody at school who didn't like them, or told me how much they hated school, their teacher, their shoes, math, their freckles, and other things. I'll have to find a new way to spend time with them when they're older, but I hope they'll always remember bedtime as special."

The Seasons

The changing seasons afford a wonderful opportunity to create a tradition to celebrate the wonders of Mother Nature. What might start out as a simple drive in the country to view the autumn colors can evolve into a wonderful everyday celebration. Theresa and her daughters have always welcomed the solstices and equinoxes. "These seasonal celebrations fit in well with home schooling and our own little family traditions. We have a set of teacups with little mice and herbs and wildflowers painted on them, one for summer, autumn, winter, and spring, and the girls also have a book for each season that goes with them. This year the girls picked fresh chamomile and four different mints to make our tea, then we took a blanket out to the backyard and sat in between my herb beds to read the appropriate book." Theresa's idea can be re-created with or without the tea.

Although spontaneous activities with just moms and daughters can be memorable and fun, it's also helpful to have someone else organize the events. Here are a few ideas that might spark your interest:

- *Celebrate summer outdoors, away from the city. Check with your local or nearby Park and Recreation Department or Fish and Game Department. Many sponsor free children's outdoor activities that include parents.*
- *Many small communities and large farms have autumn festivals to usher in the holiday season, offering pumpkin patches, hay mazes, hot apple cider, and more. Check with your state university extension office or local newspaper.*

- *Winter is a time to play in the snow, experience a real sleigh ride, or learn to ski or snowboard. If you don't live in or near snow country, you can still enjoy spending time outdoors when a winter chill is in the air.*
- *Spring is a perfect time to visit gardens or nearby farms and ranches. Check with your local nursery, gardening club, or farmer's market. If you live in or near the country, arrange to visit a farm where you and your daughter can get hands-on lessons in bottle-feeding lambs or gathering eggs, seeing how cheese is made or taking a pony ride.*

School Days

School fills a good portion of the lives of children. That's a great reason to integrate everyday celebrations with school days. Marla is in her late twenties and has two daughters, Chelsea, age eight, and MacKenna, four. "Chelsea is in second grade and loves school. We always make a really big deal of shopping for school. We designate one day as 'back-to-school day,' and get up at the same time we would if it really were a school day. We have a special breakfast, then head off to the store for school supplies, backpack, lunch box, and other supplies. I always buy a few extras as a surprise, like pencils with her name on them, a special notebook, or a little package of stickers. Then we have lunch out wherever she wants, finish shopping, and head home. Next, we make a 'back-to-school' cake, and Chelsea helps me prepare her favorite dinner. Afterward, we have the special cake and she opens her extra surprises that I bought earlier in the day. We did this for kindergarten and first grade, and she loves it."

Chris also combines school work with everyday celebrations: "I am very lucky, because even though my kids are older (my youngest is fourteen and a true blessing) I am still a stay-at-home mom. That gives me the luxury of time. We have a rule in our house that when report cards come out, and they're good, they earn a 'mental health day' as long as there isn't a test or something important scheduled. We play hooky and drive over the Peace Bridge to Niagara-on-the-Lake, have a picnic lunch at Queens Park, and pick lilacs along the roadside. Our quilt and picnic basket are always in the van, and we pack sandwiches or stop and get fresh rolls from our favorite bakery, and sharp Canadian cheddar cheese. We bring homemade lemonade from lemons I squeeze and freeze in February and March, when they're cheapest. Sometimes even kids need a day off just for fun."

Rainy Day Box

Deborah, a university professor who also knits and weaves, has found a way to turn a gloomy, rainy day into an everyday celebration for her seven-year-old daughter, Sarah: "I started filling a box with raw materials for rainy day projects—little bits of fabric, yarn, colored paper, Styrofoam, glitter, sparkly things, buttons, catalogs, different kinds of paint, markers, and other things. Sarah has been bugging me about delving into it, and it's going to be tough keeping her away from the box until that rainy day comes along."

When I was little, my mother used to make me paper dolls—not when it was raining, but just because I wanted her to. She would draw the figure of a woman on the brown cardboard from the back of a tablet of paper, then draw pretty outfits on white paper (including square tabs, so I could attach the clothing to the doll). It would take her only a half hour or so, but I would spend hours coloring the doll and her clothes, cutting them out with scissors that had rounded tips, and making up stories for the doll and me to play. Such activities, too, can be part of a rainy day tradition.

A rainy day box can be a great way to entertain your daughter if she's home sick from school, to lift her out of the doldrums, to cure boredom, or to spend quality time together. That's the key to a rainy day box—fill it with things you can do together. Here are a few more ideas:

- *Supplies for trying new hairstyles—satin and grosgrain ribbons, rubber bands, tortoiseshell combs, headbands, pretty barrettes, and a how-to book for fancy styles like chignons, French braids, and twists.*
- *Puzzles, board and card games, jacks, and a long jump rope.*
- *Supplies to create a one-of-a-kind umbrella by using fabric pens or paints to make a picture on an opened, solid-colored umbrella.*
- *Containers filled with old beads, sequins, buttons, fabric and felt scraps, pipe cleaners, Popsicle sticks, and other notions. Add a bottle of glue and some construction paper if you want to make a collage or a free-form sculpture.*
- *An empty album to fill with photographs or mementos, paste, corner tabs for photos, two-sided tape, and pens with colored ink.*

Surprise Day Trips

It can be harder to spend time with teenage daughters than with younger ones, but Paula, a high school teacher and the mother of two teenage daughters, Dawn and Brenda, has found a great way to create those close memories. "About a year ago, I noticed my daughters drifting away from me. When I tried to spend time with them, about the only thing they wanted to do was go shopping or to the movies. One Saturday, I woke them up with a surprise—we were going out for brunch to Cezanne's, a favorite restaurant on the beach in Santa Cruz, an hour's drive away. They grumbled a lot about having to get up, but we enjoyed the drive and ended up walking along the pier, watching the surfers, and *not* shopping!

I've planned a half dozen 'morning surprises' since then, and the girls look forward to them."

Grown-Up Daughters

There are plenty of reasons why adult daughters and their mothers should have everyday celebrations, too. Lisa, a mom in her late twenties, has a close relationship with her mother, Gwen. Something that started as an afterthought years ago has truly become an everyday celebration for them.

"About five years ago on a Sunday, my mom and I were driving home after having lunch together. We passed a beautiful home we'd both often admired, and noticed a realtor's Open House sign on the lawn. We looked at each other at the same time and knew we were both thinking the same thing—*I wonder what that house looks like inside?* We both love to decorate, and we decided it might be fun to tour a home that was obviously out of our price range. We explained to the realtor that we were just looking and spent an hour exploring a decorator's dream. Now we make such tours part of our go-out-to-lunch routine, which used to occur every month or so but now happens more often. We've discovered something we enjoy doing together, and it doesn't cost a dime."

Although this might seem to be an unusual way to spend time together, Lisa and Gwen simply identified something they both liked to do and decided to do it together. With some thought and imagination, I'm sure you can come up with something you have in common with your mother or daughter.

Keep in Mind

- *Everyday celebrations can happen when you least expect them.*

- *They're usually (but not always) outside your regular routine, so take a step in a new direction and see where it takes you.*
- *When something special does happen, take a moment to remember what made it so special, then re-create the situation—or come as close as you can.*
- *Look back to your own childhood and discover what you consider everyday celebrations (like my paper dolls). Can you make that "special something" a new tradition with your daughter?*
- *When you find those memories, be sure to let your mother know how important they were to you then— and now.*

PART THREE

Heritage Skills

Chapter 8

A Stitch in Time

Over the years, quilts have been valued as an expression of a mother's love, a grandmother's values, and a daughter's desire to connect with feminine culture. Quilts are beauty, romance, a place to be close, and a garden of soft pastels or rich, bold colors. When a woman makes a quilt, she's creating a legacy of comfort, dreams, memories, and tradition that transcends time and gives her the opportunity to speak to women across generations.

Quilting techniques were first used in garments and have been recovered in Egyptian tombs, worn by Mongol warriors, and made by wives during the Crusades for their husbands to wear under heavy chain mail. The use of quilted clothing and bedding quickly spread to all social classes, who used differing qualities of fabrics and threads. Generally, cotton or linen was used by the lower classes, while the elite used silk, velvet, lace, and brocade.

In Great Britain and early America, quilt making was so much a part of family life that young girls made quilts for their future homes. It was thought that a bride should have thirteen quilts, each one a different design but all following traditional family patterns. Girls as young as seven or eight started with simple themes and patterns, moving on to the more intricate designs as they grew older. On the day of her betrothal, a woman started making the thirteenth quilt, called the bride's quilt. Of course, it was the most intricately made and beautifully designed.

In Great Britain, women in different areas of the country created their own distinctive designs. Today, you'll find that those designs are still being used by their great-great-granddaughters.

Whether their patterns are geometric, inspired by nature, or represent a woman's life story told in stitches, quilts are a powerful demonstration of how traditions are bequeathed through creativity.

Look through family memorabilia for family quilt patterns. Check scrapbooks, journals, photo albums, and boxes and trunks stored in attics and basements. Talk to relatives and ask them to describe quilt patterns they might remember from childhood, or quilts that their grandmothers and great-grandmothers might have talked about.

Women have always used quilts for charitable purposes and fund-raisers, especially in times of war. The Civil War seems to have been the time of greatest quilt making because, in many cases, soldiers had to provide their own blankets. Many a soldier went off to war with a quilt made by his mother, wife, or daughter tucked into his bedroll. After the war, quilts were made using fabrics from the uniforms of returning and lost soldiers, some inscribed with names, dates, and battles.

Quilters also hand-sewed their names and the year the quilt was made along one edge. Such a signature might even tell you something about the maker.

- *Are the letters tiny and feminine or sewn in bold, bright initials?*
- *Look at the pattern—does it give you a feeling for the woman who cut the pieces and sewed them together?*
- *Did she select an old, traditional pattern or follow her own creative muse?*
- *Did she take fabric from beloved but worn garments to create something entirely new, and if so, do the fabrics tell you anything about her life?*
- *Did she design the quilt with a color scheme or a theme in mind? Take a close look, then look again from across the room. Sometimes those two viewpoints can give very different impressions.*

Quilted blankets were originally made to keep families warm on frosty winter nights. But as women stitched, they sewed love into each scrap of fabric, and as they created more intricate designs and patterns, they created memories to warm their families' hearts. While sleeping under a quilt created in an earlier time, whether that time was ten years ago or two hundred, you can connect with your heritage. Even if you didn't know your grandmother very well, you can get to know her through the quilts she stitched. If she passed the tradition of quilt making to your mother, who then passed it on to you, you're in luck. If not, you might consider yourself even luckier. You have the opportunity to start a new tradition of quilts with your mother or daughter.

Feelings about quilts can run as deeply through quilters' lives as traditions do through some families. Terry, a graphic designer, inherited her grandmother's love of quilting and has even had her quilting designs published in leading magazines. "When my mother died, she specified that I take my great-grandmother's quilt. It's a Depression quilt, made from scraps from the WPA sewing project where my grandmother worked making clothing for the families of those who were out of work. The fabrics are bright and like new, the hand quilting intricate and fine. My mother considered it one of her most cherished possessions left to her by the grandmother who took her in and helped raise her."

Terry treasures the tradition of quilting started by her grandmother, who passed it on to her mother and then herself. She says, "It's something to carry into the future, remembering stories and hearing [my ancestors'] voices in the work they did." When Terry told me about her grandmother, I knew there were life lessons to be learned from quilters by those who would listen, and wisdom to be passed on by those who understood the importance of traditions. Terry's grandmother found a way to reach the women in her family who came after her through her quilting, and she taught them the importance of working hard, caring for people, and using resources you have at hand.

You can continue the tradition of heirloom quilting by collecting small fabric samples from friends and relatives. Once you've learned the basics, design and sew a *remembrance* quilt.

Styles and Techniques

Over time, two primary methods of quilting have evolved: pieced and appliqué. Pieced (or patchwork) quilts, consisting of bits of cloth in many different shapes and sizes sewn together, have always been the most popular style. Appliqué is considered more ornamental than functional; in appliqué designs shapes are sewn to a single top layer of fabric, which is traditionally white. The appliquéd motifs are sometimes stuffed with cotton batting to give them extra dimension, and then the quilt top is layered and quilted as usual.

Quilts consist of three layers: a decorative top, batting for warmth in the middle, and a backing. Many fibers can be used for both the top and the backing: wool, linen, silk, cotton, and synthetic fabrics. The middle layer consists of a fluffy "batt" made from wool, cotton, or polyester. Fortunately, quilting techniques are relatively easy to learn and require only basic supplies (a hard working surface, needles, thread, templates, and scissors). Whether you prefer the vibrant colors and geometric designs of Amish quilts, the intricate patterns and designs of the eighteenth century, ethereal white-on-white appliqués, or more contemporary patterns, each quilt is a celebration of the endeavors and memories of the woman who created it.

Crazy Quilts

Although hundreds of pieced patterns have been created throughout quilting's history, the crazy quilt was an example of true creativity. There was no color scheme, pattern, or standards, so no two crazy quilts were alike. And because they required so much hand work, they were often made as smaller lap robes or were used to decorate a front parlor. They first appeared in Victorian times, and might have become popular because women's lives in other areas were governed by strict codes of behavior—crazy quilting let women express themselves freely, which was unthinkable in the late 1800s. They are usually heavily embroidered, so these quilts were used more for display than function, and many have survived.

Karen, a professional caterer, loves the small crazy quilt her grandmother made entirely of silk scraps from dresses, silk souvenirs, cigar bands, and what appears to be a wedding gown. The quilt is lavishly embellished throughout with embroidery and tiny beads. Karen's mother displayed the quilt inside a glass-topped coffee table until the day she surprised Karen by giving it to her. "It wasn't even a special occasion, like a birthday or Christmas. I'd gone over to Mom's for lunch, and we were having tea in the living room. I started talking about the quilt and how much I'd always loved it. She took the cups and saucers off the coffee table, took out the quilt, and gave it to me. She said it was time I got to enjoy the quilt as much as she had. I was thrilled! It took me the longest time to decide where to put it, but I finally draped the quilt across the top of our piano. A few weeks later, I decided I wanted to learn to quilt, and asked Mom if she wanted to join me. There's a shop in town that advertised quilting fabrics, and when we discovered they had lessons we signed up for a six-week course. My grandmother died before she could teach Mom to quilt, but we've carried on the tradition in remembrance of her."

Theme Quilts

Quilts have been used throughout history to celebrate events and relationships. Experts can usually tell when and where most quilts were created because of the themes and fabric used, and how the quilts were made.

Here are a few examples of themes you might want to consider:

- *If you live in Kansas, you might make a Sunflower quilt.*
- *If you're a New Englander, you might choose the pattern Ocean Waves.*
- *If the Southwest is your home, you're likely to choose cool cotton fabrics.*
- *Women in northern states would probably choose warm flannels or wool.*

If you can't find a family history of quilts, you might want to research patterns that were traditional in the area where your ancestors lived. Colors, designs, and materials differ greatly throughout the world due to climate, culture, religion, and other factors.

Carolyn and her husband developed another great way to create a theme quilt. They both have parents who've celebrated their seventy-fifth wedding anniversaries. Carolyn loves making quilts, so she sent quilt squares to friends of both her parents and her in-laws, asking them to somehow put a remembrance on the square. Most wrote their names and a greeting, but some also stitched a scene that would represent a special time they'd spent together. Once she had all the quilt squares, Carolyn made anniversary quilts for each couple.

Friendship Quilts

When Americans started moving west in the 1800s, friendship quilts became especially popular. Also called "autograph" or "album" quilts, they reflected the separation of friends and family. These quilts were especially cherished because they included hand-sewn blocks, each signed with its maker's name and often with a date, location, poetry, Bible verse, or some personal note of her relationship to the recipient. In fact, friendship quilts are considered by some experts to be the precursor to the modern autograph album. The women who created these quilts left a clear memory of themselves in their stitches and in their requests to "forget me not." As the pioneers left their friends and families for an uncertain future on the frontier, quilts provided a link with loved ones they might never see again. Although families were torn apart by distance, quilts became a bridge between the past and the future, linking generations together. Quilts continue to act as symbols of our heritage, as they did a century ago.

Jeri, an executive secretary, treasures the friendship quilt that was given to her great-grandmother, Margaret, when her family set out on the Oregon Trail. The quilt has been passed down to the women in Jeri's family, finally coming to rest with her. Each square has the name of the quilter; some have dates; some have flowers, birds, or other embellishments; and most have expressions of love and friendship. Two that Jeri especially likes are "Praying for your safe journey. Your friend and companion, Harriet," and "May you find your heart's desire. Rosalee Fisher." Jeri's ancestors eventually settled in Oregon, where her great-grandmother married and raised seven children.

Appliqué Quilts

Sometimes a quilter is unaware of how her legacy will impact the next generation and those beyond. Harriet Powers, born a slave in Georgia in 1837, created two quilts using traditional African appliqué techniques, biblical references, local legends, and astronomical phenomena. Harriet sold her quilts to a white woman named Jennie Smith who valued them highly and kept them in her family. Today, Harriet Powers's quilts hang in the Smithsonian Institution.

When Pam's daughter announced her engagement, Pam wanted to make her a quilt filled with memories. Years before, Pam's daughter had spent a year in Japan as an exchange student, and her host mother had given Pam a kimono—a gift from mother to mother. "It was one of those things you would never wear, but it was an interesting piece, and the fabric was fabulous. I ferreted in the fabric stash and made up two small foundation-pieced kimonos from Japanese fabric, added batting and a plain fabric backing, then appliquéd them on the front of the cotton kimono. I appliquéd the happy couple's initials on the front band of the kimono and printed some profound sayings on white fabric and appliquéd it onto the front. I painted a pole in burgundy red and hung the kimono outstretched with a heavy block tassel down the front." At the reception, Pam asked all the guests to write their greetings to the bride and groom on the kimono in indelible ink. The quilt now hangs in the newlyweds' entry hall and will surely be a talking point for many a guest.

Memory Quilts

Phyllis learned to sew as a child and has enjoyed making quilts for over twenty years. Her favorite projects were always made for her two daughters, Erin and Amy, and every time she looks at the pink quilt on her bed, she's reminded of them. Phyllis always dressed her girls in pretty shades of pink, and she saved their dresses, knowing one day she'd use the fabric to make a memory quilt. The pink quilt, along with all the others, will be passed down to her daughters. Phyllis was particularly pleased that Erin took along her favorite quilt when she left home for college. Erin knew she'd be homesick, and she wanted to remember her mother every day.

Debbie has two teenage daughters, Carrie and Kelly. She made memory quilts for her girls much as Phyllis did, adding fabric from the nightgowns their great-grandmother had made when the girls were toddlers. Debbie took her quilting tradition a step further when she made a memory quilt for a dear friend's baby shower. She let Carrie and Kelly choose pieces from the baby clothes, pajamas, and receiving blankets that Debbie had saved, to piece together for the quilt. "When the mother-to-be-opened the box, there was a chorus of oohs, and aahs, then Kelly told the story about the patches being from their clothing and infant pajamas."

There are many times when quilts can provide a sense of quiet and calm in a hurried, modern life. When a young mother wraps her baby in a quilt that her mother gave to the child on its day of birth, it can both soothe the child *and* bring a sense of calm to a mother worried about her new responsibilities. There are also times when your life might be filled with turmoil, grief, or sadness—times when you might need comfort and a sense that everything will be all right with the world—maybe not now, but soon. Grieving can be a time of almost overwhelming sorrow, and sometimes we feel like things were left unfinished, especially if we lose a loved one without warning.

Mourning Quilts

Mourning quilts are found throughout the world. Marni, who has welcomed two adopted children into her family and is a professional artist, says, "Having lost both my parents many years ago, I know that grief takes longer to deal with than any other emotion I have ever felt, and that it resurfaces periodically through the years even after the worst of it is over. Several years ago, I heard a hospice doctor and grief counselor on the radio talking about the things we need to say to our dying loved ones. Since my parents were already dead at the time I heard the interview, I made a quilt, and in the quilt said these things to my mother, in particular, since her death left me with some unresolved feelings: *I love you, Thank you, I forgive you, Please forgive me,* and *Good-bye.*"

The journey through grief can be difficult, and solace and comfort can seem long in coming. Marni chose to reach out with her heart—and her hands—dealing with grief through creative expression.

Decorating with Quilts

Quilts are often used as room decorations, whether hung on a wall, folded on a quilt stand, or draped over a headboard in order to complement bed linens.

Karen used her grandmother's floral bouquet bridal quilt as the focus of her bedroom by displaying the quilt on a wall. She decorated the room in closely matching pastels, using striped fabric for the drapes and solid colors for the bed. Karen finds the bedroom to be the most peaceful, intimate room in her house.

If you have an old family quilt languishing in a cupboard, find a way to incorporate it into your decor by throwing it over a chair or displaying it in a pretty basket.

Ranny has been quilting for twenty years—and working part-time in a fabric store both for inspiration and to help defray the cost of her self-proclaimed "fabric addiction." She couldn't seem to interest her daughter in quilting because Heather "thought cutting big pieces into small pieces and sewing small pieces into large pieces made about as much sense as driving backward on the freeway." So Ranny gave up, hoping one day Heather would change her mind.

Years later, when Heather was decorating her first apartment, she mentioned that she wanted a wall hanging for the stairwell. Ranny saw her chance, and showed Heather how to piece and quilt a wall hanging. A few days after they completed the project, Heather called to say, "That was sneaky, Mom. Now I'm hooked on quilting!" This family's quilting tradition is now in its third generation. Heather's daughter, Beth, is only nine, but she's already working on an Amish-inspired Center Diamond quilt for her bed. She isn't going to decorate with the quilt, though—she's planning on sleeping under it.

Quilts can be innovative as well as traditional, and are displayed in many contemporary art museums and galleries. Quilts can be made in any color of the rainbow or all of them, in many patterns and designs, and in many types of fabrics. They come in traditional motifs, geometric patterns, abstract designs, and contemporary themes. Quilts are made to commemorate people, places, and events; to please the artistic soul of the quilter; or because the quilter had to do *something* with a box of fabric scraps.

Although quilting was originally done only by hand, with a standard of twelve tiny stitches per inch, many of today's quilters sew by machine and produce wonderful results. Remember, the importance of quilts isn't the fabric or style, or whether it's hand stitched or machine made. The importance is the saving and savoring of memories. Whether traditional or contemporary in style, a quilt can be both an expression of creativity and a desire to nurture. Bring this expression into your home, your life, and the traditions you share with your mother or daughter. Here are just a few ideas to get you going:

- *Start a quilting study group with a few women friends. Explore the different types of quilts, their history, and the women who created them.*
- *Quilts can be seen in museums, art galleries, and shows and exhibits featuring textile arts. Invite your daughter or mother (or both) to go along to spark your imagination and creativity.*
- *Pick up a few magazines on quilting, both for articles and the how-to sections, complete with patterns. A good bookstore should have three or four magazines to choose from, or you might want to check your public library for both magazines and books.*
- *Take a quilting class. Check with fabric or craft stores for workshops in your area. If you're intimidated by the thought of making a quilt, start small by making a pillow, a wall hanging, a lingerie case, pot holders, placemats, a table runner, or napkins.*
- *Join a quilting circle of women who meet once every week or two to sew together. Check local fabric stores and quilt shops for contacts.*
- *Join the National Quilting Association (410-461-5733*

or on-line at www.NQAQuilts.org). It has a listing of guilds across the country, publishes a quarterly magazine, and holds an annual quilt show.

- *Join an Internet E-mail list or forum focused on quilting. The World Wide Quilting Page is a good place to start and can be found at www.ttsw.com/MainQuiltingPage.html. Information, links, and interesting related sites can also be found at www.dmoz.org/Arts/Crafts/Quilting/ and www.quilting.about.com/hobbies/quilting/.*
- *Make <u>collecting</u> quilts a tradition—invite your mother or daughter to accompany you for an afternoon excursion to country estate sales or specialty shops.*

Chapter 9

Sewing Basket

Generations of mothers and daughters have shared the experience of teaching and learning different forms of needle arts. In earlier times, needlework was an integral part of a woman's life from early childhood. As part of their education, young girls learned to sew and embroider samplers, household linens, bedding, and clothing. Most evenings were spent working quietly by the light of a fire or an oil lamp with scissors, needle, and thread. Women and young girls were proficient in making lace collars and shawls, cutting patterns from muslin, stitching clothing by hand, mending, and darning.

At the age when our daughters are playing on swing sets, young girls in earlier times were sewing dowries to prepare for marriage. By demonstrating their skill in needle arts, girls proclaimed their abilities as wives and homemakers. By the time young girls were of marriageable age, they were expected to have all the linens, bedclothes, and kitchen cloth goods needed to establish a home, as well as the ability to make their own clothing and apparel for their families. For generations, women have managed domestic matters for their families and homes, and that tradition continues today.

Machine Sewing

When I was a young girl, my mother would often come home from work and announce that she wanted something new to wear. Off we'd go to one of my favorite places—the fabric store. I was fascinated by all the bolts of material in hundreds of colors and patterns. But what I enjoyed most was running my fingers over the different materials, getting a sense of density, texture, and character. I was definitely a tactile kid.

When we came home, my mother could hardly wait to unwrap the fabric and start working—no matter how late in the evening it was. She did all her sewing in the den, where we also watched television, worked on craft projects, or played Monopoly, Scrabble, or Canasta. My mother was a wonderfully dedicated seamstress, and once she started a project she rarely stopped until she finished, even if that meant getting only a few hours of sleep. When I went to bed she might still be cutting out the pattern, but when I woke up the next morning she'd have a new skirt, jacket, or dress to wear to work that day.

By the time I was ten those trips to the fabric store were as much for me as for my mother. I was in the seventh grade the first time I designed and made my own clothing. We lived in Arizona then, and since summer weather lasted through October, I wanted to make some lightweight school clothes. I decided on two skirts and blouses that were interchangeable—one set in pale blue cotton, the other in a matching blue-and-white seersucker.

Learning to sew gave me a sense of empowerment. I came up with an idea, chose colors and textures to complement the design, fitted the pattern, and did the work myself. My mother let me learn at my own pace, allowed me free rein when it came to style, and gave little criticism and lavish praise. She didn't hover over me or take over when she knew I was off track. She let me make mistakes and learn from them. I still remember the problem with my first design attempt—the armholes on the sleeveless blouses were too low. Since I'd cut out the fabric pieces for both blouses before beginning to sew, I learned (the hard way) that you should always fit a pattern to your body *before* making that first cut.

Many mothers and daughters who sew have fond memories of both making dresses and developing pride in their creations, not to mention the new bond they were forming. Shelly remembers watching her mother sew a dress for her: "It was a powder blue jumper with a little embroidered teddy bear. I remember wearing it to school and having my first home economics teacher say to me how cute the dress was. I can remember how proud I felt telling the teacher that my mother had made it. I loved that dress. Now, I have a little girl, and I can remember every outfit I've made for her. Each outfit was made with love—just like the powder blue jumper my mother made for me. I can see the same pride in Katie. When someone compliments her on an outfit, she says with a smile, 'My mommy made it, and I feel like I'm on top of the world.

"Now that she's seven, I'm teaching Katie to sew. As I watch her patiently working a row of stitching on her little square of fabric, I hope she will remember fondly this time spent with me. When she shows me what she has accomplished, with a face glowing with pride, I remember back to when I showed my grandmother and mother all that I made. I kiss Katie and praise her work, just as they kissed and praised me."

Shelly describes her experience this way: "Something wonderful happens when you learn to sew, knit, or embroider. You learn patience. You become creative and imaginative. You get pleasure in giving a handmade gift to a family member or friend."

Most women have a history of needlework somewhere in their families. Geri, a professional consultant, figures her seamstress ancestry goes all the way back to before slavery. Geri's mother took her sewing skills and parlayed them from working in a sewing factory to a degree in home economics. Geri remembers following her mother through stores as a child, feeling the clothes and having her mother reprimand her until she realized Geri was imitating her. That's when she started showing Geri how to feel the fabric to determine its quality. Geri's love affair with textiles, like mine, seems to be an inherited trait.

As a child, Connie first sewed clothes for her Barbie doll, and when she grew up she went on to make her own clothing. She still loves to sew, and decided to start her daughter, Hannah, off with a needle and thread early on. When Hannah turned four, Connie

Drawstring Bag

¼ to ½ yard fabric
Matching thread
12 to 18 inches ribbon,
    ½ inch wide

Cut two pieces of fabric the same size and shape you want the bag. Put right sides together and hand-sew or machine-sew securely around three sides, leaving the top open. Turn the bag inside out. Fold fabric down and to the inside to form a 1″ hem around the opening. Stitch the hem closed, leaving a 2″ gap at one end. Attach a small safety pin to one end of the ribbon and insert it through the opening, threading the safety pin (and ribbon) along the hem and out the other side of the opening. Remove the safety pin, trim the ends of the ribbon, and tie the bag closed with a bow.

found a simple project they could do together. It was an alphabet pillow with the letter *H*. "We pulled out the *H,* and I helped Hannah pin it down to some darling white flannel covered with pastel-colored bows and ribbons. Then she cut it out all by herself and it was time for us to sew on the machine. I had her sit in my lap while she guided the fabric, but she desperately wanted to push the foot pedal herself, so I decided to give it a whirl and let her sit in my chair. She could scoot way to the end of the chair and reach the pedal with her foot, and I helped her guide the fabric while she pressed the pedal. She was so proud. Then we went to Wal-Mart to get stuffing for the pillow. I couldn't help but smile when she told the salesclerk, 'I'm a real mommy now because I can sew.' "

At the left is an easy sewing project for a little girl—a drawstring bag in which she can keep her collection of marbles, jewelry, or anything else small.

Handwork

Although my daughter didn't take to sewing on a machine, she does enjoy handwork (which includes needlepoint, crewel, petit point, applique, embroidery, all types of lacemaking, and any sewing done by hand). She's currently making colorful Christmas stockings for her niece and nephew. So, if you aren't successful at your first try at teaching a daughter to sew, cross-stitch, or embroider, don't give up. There are many skills that utilize a thread and needle, and you're sure to find one that suits you and your daughter.

Take Celeste, for instance. She is a psychologist by training and a stay-at-home mom by choice. She has five sisters, and her mother taught each of them some form of needlework. For a mother of a large family, she didn't cook very much, choosing to express her creative streak in needlework. Celeste echoes her mother's attitude when she says, "It has always seemed a moot point to spend your whole day cooking, and then have it all eaten up, when you could spend your time sewing or knitting and have something to show for it." The sisters often joke that they were born with needles in their hands. Celeste sews and knits; Julie quilts and does hardanger lace; Annette quilts and crochets; Janine does counted cross-stitch and needlepoint; Carol knits; and Kay sews.

Celeste's mother taught her daughters the value of careful work, planning, and diligence. When Celeste sits down today, she thinks of her mother and usually picks up something to do with her hands. Whether sewing, knitting, or planning the next project, those memories are a steadfast reminder of the traditions passed along by her mother.

When Michelle was planning her wedding last year, she wanted to make something special for her mother: "When I saw the cross-stitch pattern of a mother and daughter on the morning of the daughter's wedding day, I knew it was the perfect gift. The daughter is standing in front of a mirror in her wedding gown and the mother is helping fix her veil. But as the mom looks in the mirror, she sees not her grown daughter but a memory of when her daughter was a young girl. I thought it would be a touching memory for both Mom and me."

One way to ignite your daughter's passion for handwork is the gift of a sewing box. Holly, a textile enthusiast who raises Shetland sheep and Angora rabbits, vainly tried to pass on her sewing heritage to her daughter, Bethany. Bethany frequently watched her mother sewing and had done a bit of felt sewing herself, so Holly thought the time was right. On Bethany's fifth birthday, Holly gave her a fully stocked sewing box. Bethany wasn't as interested in sewing as Holly thought, and Holly made the wise decision to not push her. "It was fully two years later before Bethany finally started showing a real interest, and that was when she reread the Little House in the Prairie series. I think she decided that if Laura could sew quilt blocks, so could she. I gave her a bunch of bright colored squares left over from a project, and she began using the tools in her box and sewing them together by hand."

It's easy to put together a sewing box for your daughter. You can find boxes at fabric and craft stores. Choose a pretty one and fill it with things that are both useful and that might spark her imagination: a variety of cotton and metallic threads, cotton and silk embroidery floss in her favorite colors, several packages of pretty beads or seed pearls, scissors for handwork (small) and for pattern work (medium or large), a thimble, a measuring tape, a pincushion, pins, and needles for hand and machine sewing, embroidery, and beading. A gift certificate for fabric would be an especially nice touch.

In the eighteenth century, women often made tokens of friendship to give to each other. Many of these small gifts were lavishly embroidered with silk threads, but many were also made with scraps of fabric and ribbons the women had at hand. Pincushions, needle cases, bookmarks, handkerchiefs, and sachets were among the small gifts women personalized with initials, names, flowers, and sayings such as "Friendship," "Love," or "Remember Me." Some were done in needlepoint, others embroidered, cross-stitched or simply sewn by hand. The tradition of giving handmade gifts transcends the value of items you might purchase. It's a reminder of a place and time, those you cherish, or an event with particular meaning.

There are instructional books and videos to make learning or teaching embroidery relatively simple, and you can create a lovely piece by using just two or three basic stitches. Embroidery hoops, floss, and preprinted projects are inexpensive and available at stores that offer fabric, craft, and general merchandise. If you already know how to embroider, you might be ready to design your own pattern, stitches, and colors for a truly unique piece.

Heirloom Sewing

There has been a renewed interest in heirloom sewing over the last few years, so much so that many pieces are now considered *collectible*. Original articles from a hundred years ago would include fine linens and bedding, lingerie, day and evening clothing, accessories, and christening and wedding gowns. The materials used for heirloom projects are of the highest-quality natural fibers such as linen, silk, cotton, and wool. The workmanship is also the finest, always done by hand using time-honored techniques such as tiny, precise stitches and rolled or whipped edges. Design elements might include tiny tucks and pleats, smocking, lace insets, decorative hand stitching, and beading. Some other things to look for are mother-of-pearl buttons, enameled pins with floral designs, embroidered medallions, French ribbons, silk or eyelet embroidery, and fine lace the color of good champagne.

My Great-Aunt Jessie tatted lace to the edges of pillowcases to give to the unmarried girls in our family. Those pillowcases, along with hand-embroidered linens passed down in my family through the years, are among my most treasured heirlooms. If you, your mother, and your daughter have fallen in love with the idea of owning heirloom handwork and won't be inheriting any, you can still acquire pieces in antiques stores, from vintage clothing shops, and at estate sales.

With today's sewing machines, you can even replicate yesterday's fine hand-sewing techniques with excellent results in a fraction of the time. You might decide to try your hand at true heirloom sewing by duplicating the materials and craftsmanship of yesterday. A few small, easy-to-make items that would work

Lace Sachet

¼ yard lace
¼ yard tulle netting
Lingerie-weight thread the
   same color as the lace
2 to 4 ounces scented potpourri

Cut two pieces of lace to the desired size. Place the same size tulle netting on the wrong side of each piece of lace, and baste along the edges. With right sides together, stitch the pieces of lace together along three sides, ¼ inch from the edge. Turn right side out. Fill the sachet with potpourri and whipstitch the opening closed. Trim by whipstitching gathered lace trim along the seam line of all four sides.

well for a first project are lace-edged handkerchiefs, sachets, pillow slips with embroidered ruffles, or monogrammed linen guest towels.

The act of creating something for someone you care about is a symbol of enduring love. A blend of your personal artistry and workmanship with a sense of intimacy is an inherent part of any handmade gift. It's a tradition we should cherish, follow, and keep in the family. Here's how:

- *Join the American Sewing Guild (816-444-3500 or on-line at www.asg.org) or the Embroiderer's Guild of America (502-589-6956 or on-line at www.egausa.org), which have chapters across the country in large cities, towns, and neighborhoods. Guilds are a great place to meet people interested in needlework, and also hold various workshops aimed at all levels of instruction—from beginner to advanced.*

- *Teach your daughter basic sewing skills or how to embroider. If your mother has these skills, ask her to teach you.*

- *Research your ancestry to discover what your great-great-grandmother sewed one hundred years ago for her family. Were there particular colors, styles, or patterns characteristic of the area where your ancestors lived? Find out whether or not your family had a tradition of wearing distinctive clothing, such as Native American bead and leather work, Belgian lace,*

Japanese and European embroidery, Scottish tartans, or the geometrical motifs of Africa.

- *Call local museums, universities, and galleries to inquire about upcoming textile exhibits. Be sure to attend, and ask your mother, daughter, sister, or girlfriend to go with you.*

- *Pick up some magazines devoted to sewing, embroidery, and textiles—such as* Threads, Sew News, Piecework, Cross-Stitch, *and* Needlework. *Most of them have listings of upcoming exhibits and workshops, as well as how-to articles and patterns.*

- *Buy a beginning instruction book on both hand and machine sewing for you and your daughter—for ages five to eight,* Sewing by Hand, *by Christine Hoffman; for ages eight to thirteen,* Sewing Machine Fun, *Dreamspinner Discovery Series, by Nancy Smith and Lynda Milligan; for beginner adults,* Sewing Basics— Creating a Stylish Wardrobe with Step-by-Step Techniques, *by Patricia Moyes, and* Singer—the New Sewing Essentials; *and for heirloom sewing,* Heirloom Sewing for Today, *by Sandy Hunter.*

- *A book with a good overview of needlecrafts is* The Good Housekeeping Illustrated Book of Needlecrafts. *For the more advanced student, or especially for inspiration:* The Embroiderer's Garden, *by Thomasina Beck, and* Creative Tapestry Designs, *by Jill Gordon.*

Chapter 10

Weaving Life's Tapestry

The ancient philosopher Plato applied the analogy of spinning and weaving with the forces of life, death, and rebirth in his vision of the great goddess Ananke spinning the universe, the sun, the moon, and the planets. In a similar fashion, our female ancestors have spun fibers to create thread and yarn, then gone on to create the structured material needed to produce clothing for their families and furnishings for their homes. In many ways, textiles and fiber crafts have been inexorably intertwined with a woman's expression of devotion to her loved ones and a symbol of her family's legacy.

In certain cases, some women involved with primary textile arts such as weaving, spinning, and knitting (as opposed to sewing from finished fabric you did not make) believe there is a "textile gene" that resides deep within them. To these women, there's something that seems almost too familiar about the touch and feel of fibers and textiles, and the repetitive motions it takes to create finished products. I even know women who feel this *connection* even though they didn't learn about textiles from their mothers and discovered fiber arts through some other means.

There is so much to enjoy in the beauty that handcrafting brings to our lives, whether or not you have a "textile gene"—the satisfaction of creating something unique; the repetitive nature of working with loom, wheel, and needle; and the soothing sense of calm that comes with each pass of the shuttle, turn of the wheel, or dip of the needle. Time and troubles seem to fade away, while peace, focus, and creativity come to the forefront. Today, we also have the luxury of carrying on the tradition of fiber arts and crafts because we *want* to, not because we *must*.

If you're like most women, you're familiar with weaving and knitting only through finished products and might never have seen anyone spin or weave, unless it was through the guise of historical reenactment. Just so you won't be too intimidated by the thought of trying something that seems quite complicated, this book provides a few starting points in the hope that you will explore the community of women who teach, share, and love these traditional arts and crafts.

For a historical perspective, you might begin by reading *Women's Work: The First 20,000 Years—Women, Cloth and Society in Early Times,* by Elizabeth Wayland Barber.

Weaving

Weaving, the lacing together of threads and yarns to form cloth, has developed over thousands of years through every culture and uses a variety of fibers from plants such as cotton, hemp, and flax; diverse protein sources such as wool (sheep), mohair (goats), Angora (rabbits), and silk (cocoons made by worms); or man-made products such as acrylic and nylon. Weavers use them all.

I learned to weave a few years ago, and quite by chance. I read about a textile exhibit at an art gallery in a neighboring town, including the name of the sponsoring fiber guild. I was surprised and delighted to learn that a group of women ran a weaving studio nearby and that lessons were available for very little money. Most of these women are in their sixties and seventies, and are committed to passing along their skills to a new generation of weavers. After a few lessons, I realized weaving is more difficult than I'd imagined, and after a few years, I know one thing—I have a lot to learn!

Francine has three daughters and is a stay-at-home mom who weaves, spins, and knits. "I was blessed with an opportunity to weave with all of my daughters during the much-anticipated birth of my son. All of the girls wanted to have a hand in weaving the receiving blanket that I had put on a small table loom. It was wonderful to have my eldest on my right, pushing the levers and throwing the shuttle to her next sister, who sat on my left, catching and making sure that 'my edges are even, Mommy.' My youngest daughter, at the time not quite two, sat on my lap and did the 'Beat, beat.' It's a very special blanket as they all had a hand in making it and were able to wrap the blanket around their new brother just minutes after they had seen him born. It is not unusual in this household to see all six of us doing something craft-related together. My husband often works on jewelry with the help of at least one pair of small hands, and I often have at least one child helping me, whether I am spinning, weaving, or doing needlework of some sort. I'm blessed to be able to pass on my knowledge of the things I love to those that I love, in the same way that my mother taught me."

If you'd like to discover similar opportunities to learn to weave, here are a few suggestions for finding information about weaving studios, lessons, and supplies:

- *Call museums and galleries and ask if any textile or fiber artists display their work. Ask for contact information, and if it's not available, leave a note for the artist and ask her or him to call you.*
- *Check the yellow pages under "Yarns" or "Weaving" for retail shops and studios. You might find bulletin boards with advertisements for lessons.*
- *Some universities, colleges, and private craft centers offer classes and/or degrees in textiles and have weaving studios on campus. Check to see if one near you offers introductory courses for the public.*
- *There are many professional weavers' sites on the Internet. Go to a search engine, type in "weaving" and explore, or get on an E-mail list devoted to weavers, like www.quilt.net/weaving.html.*

- *There are several excellent weaving magazines, including* Handwoven, *available at specialty shops and large bookstores.*

Tapestry Weaving

Tapestries became popular during the Middle Ages. The upper social classes, along with a multitude of servants, lived in large manor houses or stone castles. These buildings were almost impossible to heat and were cold and damp. One way to insulate them was by hanging large tapestries on the walls. Tapestries were also used to separate large halls into smaller rooms and to cover the seats of chairs or padded footstools.

I decided to learn how to weave tapestries when I bought a small flock of Karakul sheep, a primitive breed originally from Persia that is considered an endangered breed in this country. Their fleece is long, coarse, and lustrous, and comes in wonderful colors (reddish brown, grays, black, white, rose, and pied). Although it is believed Karakuls are the source of the original felting fleece, their wool is also traditionally used to make the yarn for Persian carpets and tapestries.

Kristin, a weaver, tapestry designer, and aspiring writer, lived in Norway when she was a child. "We got to know our family, the language, and the country, and Mama had a chance to take classes in natural dyeing and weaving. Like the work of many Norwegian weavers, her first tapestries were copies of medieval pieces in the museums. She bought an upright loom and set it up in our living room to practice between classes. The first tapestry on the loom used only two thirds of the available width, which left eight or nine inches of warp free. When I asked if I could make something, too, she explained how to draw a weaving cartoon and critiqued it until we were both satisfied. Then she showed me how to wind yarn into 'butterflies' over my fingers, how to bubble the weft, how to beat it down with a fork, and how to tie rya knots over a school pencil to make a flossa horse and cloud on a plain-weave ground. Weaving that little horse was the most exciting thing I had ever done, and I knew I had to be a weaver. I remember her standing behind me, patting my back now and then, and saying, 'Breathe. You have to breathe.' I was thirteen.

"While doing graduate work in clothing and textiles at Oregon State, I fell in love with weaving all over again—this time I attempted table linens and a rug on a countermarch loom. I spent long days in the woods and mountains finding dye plants, especially lichens, in researching my thesis. I told Mama about wanting to learn to use natural dyes, and we arranged for me to take a natural-dye course in Oslo, which turned out to be the same one she had audited so many years before—and with the same teacher.

"My fiber legacy from my mother and grandmothers is so much more than 'things.' Mama passed away, but her natural-dyed yarns, dyeing and weaving notebooks, tapestry cartoons, rosepath and krokbragd runners, and the upright tapestry loom I learned to weave on are still part of my life. She had gone to Norway most summers, and sometimes came across old weaving and spinning equipment that was still in good shape—a wooden ratchet wheel from an old loom, hand-tied reeds, a Finnish flax wheel from 1860, a skein winder. Once, walking on a hillside, she found a piece of granite about the size of two fists that had been carefully chipped until it was shaped like an hourglass. She was convinced it was a weight for an old warp-weighted loom. These memories are as much a part of my life as the craft my grandmother taught me."

Kathy, a tapestry artist, inherited a box of old family photos from her grandmother. "Most of the photos I have are very small, old black-and-whites. I've decided to take the image from one photo and weave it into a tapestry. It's of my grandmother and five friends at a church picnic where they are all holding watermelons. What I love about this picture is the friendship I see among these women, and the fact that my grandmother looks so much like me. I feel such a connection with this photo that it could almost be of my daughters and me preparing a meal together and sharing gossip.

"As I weave, I'm developing quite a relationship with 'my women.' They are most agreeable companions, but when I tire of them, I can simply turn out the studio lights and leave them for a while. There is another small group of photos I'm considering for a tapestry as well. They're of my parents when they were just beginning to date, playing croquet with some friends. One of the reasons I love tapestry weaving is because it's a way to tell stories with an unusual and visual technique."

Spinning

Spinning is an ancient craft that involves transforming loose fibers into thread by pulling on the fibers until they reach the desired width while introducing twist to anchor and strengthen them. Long ago, the tools used by a spinner were the distaff and the spindle. The long shaft of the distaff kept the fibers from becoming tangled, while the spindle (a short shaft weighted with a stone whorl called a drop spindle) provided momentum and the downward pull of gravity just like a suspended spinning top. Early spinning wheels were introduced in the late fourteenth century, and by the eighteenth century were in use in most modernized societies. The drop spindle is still the most widely used tool in the world to create thread and yarn, both in third-world countries and by many of today's modern spinners.

I became interested in spinning when I wanted to find uses for the wool from our sheep. Besides the Karakuls, we also raise sheep with fine and medium-grade fleeces suitable for garments worn next to the skin or as outerwear. Although some people think you should first learn to spin on a drop spindle, I tried but couldn't get the hang of it. I finally learned on a wheel, then went back a few years later to relearn spinning on a drop spindle. I love the portability of spindles and the production possibilities of the wheel. Both are equally relaxing and meditative, but there's something about taking a long walk on our acreage, lightweight spindle and some wool in hand, that transports me back in time. I have two spinning wheels, four drop spindles, a counterbalance floor loom, and several tapestry looms, and use them all for different fibers and projects. The more I delve into fiber arts and textiles, the more I want to learn.

Linda has two daughters, Crystal, eight, and Meagan, ten. When I asked her why she took up spinning, she said, "Well, to begin with, I have this hereditary disease called creativity. My mother had it, I have it, and I have passed it on to both my daughters! A few years ago, I fell in love with alpacas (related to the llamas of South America and having fine, long wool), and even worked on a farm for a while. I became intrigued by their fiber and decided to learn how to spin on a drop spindle. A few days later, I was out enjoying my summertime passion—garage sales—and found a large toy wheel drop spindle with two sandwich bags of wool for two dollars. I tried to follow the directions but couldn't make heads nor tails of them. After I picked up the girls from school, we went to the library and borrowed every book I could find on the subject, spun and dropped the spindle several times, but only managed to spin a small amount of fiber. The girls were really intrigued, as they always are when I get a new toy. Several days and a few feet of spun wool later, I met up with my friend and told her all about my troubles with this spinning thing. She suggested I give her alpaca fiber a try, and I immediately fell in love with spinning. All this time the girls kept asking, 'Can I try? Can I spin it? Please?' So I decided to teach them.

"I was pretty impressed with Meagan's ability to pick it up with help, and Crystal was just plain determined. When the girls and I decided they needed their own spindles to practice on, we put together a couple of toy wooden wheel spindles. Crystal painted the base of her spindle a baby blue and added a bouquet of pink and purple flowers. Meagan's is quite wild—she painted it white with green and orange horizontal stripes. The girls are happy, and I don't have to share my spindles anymore.

"Recently, Crystal broke her arm climbing on the monkey bars and was pretty unhappy because I told her she couldn't spin until the cast came off. A week later, while we were all waiting in Crystal's doctor's office, I decided to get some spinning done. Meagan stood in the middle of the room telling everyone what I was doing and how it was done. Crystal decided that she wanted to try, even with her cast on up to her armpit, so I gave in. There she was, drafting with her broken arm and spinning with her good one. It truly was a sight!"

There are a number of ways to find spinners, no matter where you live:

- *There are numerous E-mail lists on the Internet focused on spinning. I'm familiar with www.spinning.net, which is primarily for those spinning with a wheel, and for drop spindles: www.xws.com/terispage/spindle.html.*
- Spin-Off *magazine is great resource and available from Interweave Press, specialty shops, or large bookstores. Once a year they print a listing of all the spinning guilds in the country—and there are a lot!*
- *The Handweavers Guild of America, which consists of spinners, weavers, dyers, and basketmakers, publishes a magazine, "Shuttle, Spindle, Dyepot," and holds a large annual conference. They can be reached at 770-495-7702 or on-line at: www.weavespindye.org.*

Knitting

Knitting can be traced back to Egypt, circa 1200 to 1500 B.C. Yet the first physical representation of a woman knitting can be found in five paintings from the fourteenth century. These Italian and German paintings all represent the Christian Madonna and Child,

Easy Lacy Scarf

200 to 250 yards silk, mohair, or
    Angora yarn
Size 12 (U.S.) knitting needles
Crochet hook, any size

Cast-on 22 stitches. K2 * P1, YO, P2 together, K1. Repeat from * to end of row. Continue in this pattern until the scarf measures desired length. Bind off loosely. Fringe: cut 44 pieces of yarn twice the desired length plus one inch (for knotting). Fold the first strand in half. Insert any size crochet hook through the end stitch on one end of the scarf. Catch the fold of the strand with your hook and pull it through the hole an inch or two. Then go under the strands, catching the ends and pulling through the loop that you have just created. This creates a secure knot to hold the fringe in place. Continue adding fringe to each stitch along both ends of the scarf. Wet-block by pinning the scarf on a towel, then using a spray bottle to wet thoroughly. Allow to dry completely.

and are generally referred to as the Knitting Madonnas. Currently, there is a revival in interest in knitting. Movie stars like Julia Roberts and Winona Ryder are taking up needles and yarn along with mothers and daughters all over the country.

For a historical perspective, read *The History of Hand Knitting,* by Richard Rutt. For inspiration, patterns, and profiles on a dozen women who knit and design professionally, read *Knitting in America,* by Melanie D. Falick.

I have early memories of watching my mother knit, her needles moving steadily as she carried on a conversation or watched television. It was something she did while doing something else, and I always thought that was neat. Although I learned early, I've always kept to simple patterns rather than the intricate color weaves and designs I admire. I've also taught children to knit, and have read that experts believe that knitting helps little ones with eye and hand coordination.

A few simple projects even a beginning knitter could teach her daughter, or that you could learn together, are a drawstring purse or bag, scarf, shawl, ski hat or tam, an afghan or a crib blanket.

Kate, with degrees in linguistics and language instruction, is now a self-employed designer of knitting and needlework patterns. She doesn't remember the details about her mother teaching her to knit, but she does remember when her mom took a knitting class at the Y and showed her the new method of casting-on that she'd learned: "I also vividly remember her project, a pink cabled cardigan. When I was quite young, I pretended to teach my Barbie doll how to knit by using thin red reinforcing or mending wool on curler picks. The little bulges in the middle of the picks made it rather challenging.

"My mother and grandmother knitted socks and mittens in worsted-weight wool on small needles, making the fabric dense and warm. My grandma passed away when I was about fourteen, and I remember realizing that either I had to learn to knit socks or this tradition would come to an end. So I did. In honor of my grandma, I taught my three boys and three girls how to knit. It's 'taken' with the two younger girls, now fifteen and sixteen. Each has socks in the works, and the sixteen-year-old is also knitting a cotton top. I've always provided them with their own materials and tools, and let them choose their own yarns and projects at the needlework shop. They're pretty talented kids. I've just tried to support their efforts, let them do their thing, and be there to help if needed."

The tradition that skipped a generation suddenly began to intrigue Kate's mother, who is eighty-seven. She hadn't done any knitting in years, until she was visiting and saw some swatches Kate was working on. "I went to my stash and presented her with yarn and needles, as she had done for me so many years before. The week I taught her a new way to knit the thumb on a mitten was the same week I taught her to use E-mail."

Lynn was born in England and learned to knit in school when she was six, which began a lifelong love of knitting that she, too, shared with her mother: "The first project I decided to knit was a cable turtleneck in the round. I had been out with Mum and mentioned I wanted to try to knit something, so we went to a store than sold wool. When I chose a project requiring circular needles, she asked me if I felt up to it, because she thought I should start with something simple like a scarf. I confidently said 'Yes!' I was so excited when we went back to her apartment and got started. After I had done the ribbing, she showed me how to do the cables. Three intensive weeks and many dropped stitches later, I finished the sweater.

"I began going to my local yarn store and buying projects for Mum to knit, because I wanted to make sure she always had something on her needles. She doesn't hesitate, however, to put her work down to do a sleeve or a front for her still impatient, compulsive daughter. Together, we have knitted many gifts, including cardigans each year for her grandchildren. This past year has been very difficult for both of us. Mum is in poor health. Sometimes she works on a stocking stitch basic pullover, on better days she picks up an Aran sweater for me. We have some special sayings, too. When Mum says, 'I did a few lines tonight,' I always respond with 'It's about bloody time.' Knitting is a very special bond we have. It reminds Mum of simpler times in England, and she tells me stories about knitting on her break at the cotton mill where she worked during the war, or how her best friend and she knitted the same items while they were expecting."

I heard from Lynn again a few months later, with some sad news: "Yesterday, Mum passed away. Just a few hours earlier at her hospital bed, she checked my knitting one last time 'just to be sure the rows were right,' her fingers touching the stitches as her eyes carefully inspected them. I am so proud of her."

Knitting is probably the easiest of the traditional skills to learn and takes the least investment in equipment and supplies. Here are a few ways to find both teachers and a knitting circle of women to join:

- *Check under "Yarn" in the yellow pages and call one of the stores listed (preferably an independent shop rather than a chain retailer). Such a store is sure to have classes available at all levels of instruction, as well as the necessary supplies and advice to get you started.*
- Interweave Knits, Vogue Knitting, *and other*

magazines for knitters can be found in bookstores and knitting shops.

- *The Knitting Guild of America is a good resource for both beginners and experts. It publishes a magazine,* Cast On, *and hosts several regional conferences. Contact the guild at 800-274-6034 or on-line at www.tkga.com.*

- *A great Internet site for researching arts and crafts—including lists of guilds, magazines, and books—is www.about.com.*

- *There are a number of Internet knitting E-mail lists, including www.kniton.com/knitlist/index.html and www.knittedlace.com. You can also go to www.egroups.com, type in "knitting" and you'll find many more.*

- *Another way to access Internet sites is through a web ring, a list of web sites focusing on a similar subject (knitters, spinners, or weavers, for example). Go to www.webring.org and type in any topic in the search window for a list of sites.*

Chapter 11

Nature and Wildcrafting

The beauty in the world around us both inspires and challenges, and although we might come from different ethnic and social backgrounds, we also share a strong connection to nature. Then and now, the land nurtures and sustains life. Communing with nature reminds us that we exist in relationship to the earth and an amazing array of plants and animals. When I exchanged a successful career in a big city nine years ago for life on a farm, I made the move for the love of a man, but I also found a connection with the natural world that changed my life. As it turned out, the love of my life wasn't only the man but the rugged landscape of the Pacific Northwest he introduced me to.

My first thought about my new country home was that it was a beautiful place that dreams were made of. We drove down the long gravel driveway during the first week of April when the land was glorious with springtime. The oak trees were resplendent with bright green leaves that grew alongside majestic ponderosa pines and blue spruce. Tiny wildflowers dotted the meadows with hints of pale yellow, pink, deep purple, and white, and the pasture was lush and green with new grass. A small flock of sheep, some fluffed out in white wool, others in shades of gray or brown, raised their heads to glance at us as we drove by. I felt like I was in another world—a natural one, but one I knew little about. Now I feel like I've become part of the landscape, and the seasons call to me this year as they did last. There's an old saying that home is where the heart is, and that's certainly true for me.

If you live in the city, nature isn't usually close at hand. But don't let that stop you and your mother or daughter from getting back in touch with nature. Instead, you should all go out and find a corner of the natural world to explore together. Whether that's a train ride to the country, a day at the beach or a nearby lake, or simple picnics in the park, find a way for everyone to take that first step as a family.

- *Choose a topic from nature you and your mom know nothing about and become experts—the more unusual the subject, the better.*
- *Set up a small fish tank with your daughter. Place it on a corner table and stock it with iridescent goldfish or more exotic specimens.*
- *If you've never had fresh ranch eggs, they should be available at any health food store. Try fixing your family brown eggs, fertilized eggs, even duck eggs!*
- *Buy a recording of the sounds of nature—the ocean, thunderstorms, or the sounds of birds and insects. Listen to it with your mother and daughter, and get inspired.*

Nature Walks and Journals

Creating nature journals is easy. You take children on a nature walk and take along journals, writing utensils, and small bags to collect leaves, twigs, or anything that grabs their attention. The children sketch whatever strikes their interest and collect a hodge-podge of things to write about in their journals. Later on, show them how to press special flowers or leaves they've collected. It's great fun, educational, and good exercise.

Another good idea for nature journaling is to have the children sketch the same scene during spring, summer, fall, and winter, so they will develop an awareness of climate and its effects on animals and plant life.

Carrie's husband is in the military, and because they've moved a lot, she and her three daughters have explored many different areas of the country. The first time Carrie heard about nature journals was in a homeschool support group meeting, but she had also read about them in an out-of-print book called *Nature's Parables*, written in the mid-1800s. Carrie started the girls nature journaling when they lived in Fort Lewis, Washington, and went on a cool tidal pool home schooling field day in the Pacific Sound. "The beach rangers walked out in their waders and found all kinds of beautiful sea creatures for the children to see. The talk was wonderful, and the children were taught to look and observe. Then we walked along the beach, finding sea creatures on our own, including the most colorful sea stars I'd ever seen. We used to walk in a park that had blackberry bushes, and Sara also has a page with drawings of the flowers that ringed the outside of the bushes. Her drawings remind us of all the fun we had picking blackberries, the bee sting one of her friends got, and the jelly we made that summer. Sara also made drawings of wild mushrooms from the forested area where we sometimes walked, and has been pressing flowers (four o'clocks, morning glories, Cyprus flowers, and zinnia petals, among others), and learning all the names of the flowers that grow where we live now. I've started letting her take my camera on our walks so she can have photos of the live creatures that move too fast for her to sketch. Later, we work on identification with the books we have from the National Audubon Society.

"My grandpa's favorite tree was a huge catalpa, where he'd sit in the shade on summer evenings and read some western paperback; my grandma loved her beautiful mimosa tree with lacy pink blooms. Our new house has both catalpa and mimosa trees, so I can pass on the memories of play time in my grandma's yard to my children and watch them and the trees grow."

Night Skies

When I moved to the country, one of the most noticeable differences was the night sky. It stretched forever on a backdrop of deepest purple and black, and was peppered with thousands of stars. I'd never seen so many! If you haven't had a chance to see a night sky far away from city lights, find a way for you and your mother or daughter to experience this stark contrast to city nights.

Miriam is a retired labor coach and masseuse, and lives in a small town in Israel, which she describes as "having pure air and water, and mountain views at every turn that keep body and spirit cleaner than in the big city." During a display of Leonid meteorite showers, Miriam and her fifteen-year-old daughter, Rose, got up at four in the morning to watch. "We huddled together on the balcony, watching a sharply defined Milky Way, whose stars were eerily closer and brighter than we had ever seen. Shooting stars began slipping through the atmosphere very quickly, leaving glittery white streaks that lingered for a second or so. Rose and I kept turning around to take in the awesome proximity and brightness of the constellations, which seemed to re-create their mythical outlines and move in the night sky while shooting stars conducted their dance across the blackness.

"The eternity of the nightscape made us feel small, so Rose and I clung together. I wondered if there was a message in the stars, and if so, perhaps it was to cherish your love, for human lives are small under the heavens, and love is what goes forward into the future, linking mother to child as long as the generations survive. It had been many years since I nurtured Rose from my body, fed her, picked her up, and put her on my lap to cuddle or soothe her, yet she leaned gracefully toward me, as natural as when she was a baby. She is becoming a young woman, and I am advancing into middle age, but as long as we're both willing to get up in the middle of the night to watch a meteor shower together, we won't grow too far apart. That night was a lovely and rare thing, and experiencing it with my daughter strengthened our bond in ways I never thought possible."

Birding

Perhaps one of the easiest ways to connect with nature is through birding, or bird-watching. Jeanne, who works with children with learning disabilities, grew up with a tradition of birding. "I stayed with Gramma when my mother worked at a newspaper, so we spent a lot of time together. She took me with her to band birds once, and I remember how fragile the little bird seemed as I held it, oh so carefully, while it was banded. Then I got to release it and watch it fly up into the sky. I've always kept that love of birds, and have had the girls help me rescue orphaned chicks over the years. Stephanie loved the little parakeet we had when she was a toddler, so much so that her first word was *bird*. She was enthralled when we let it fly around the house from perch to perch.

"Whenever we went on a trip with Gramma, she was known for hollering, 'Jack, Jack, pull over quick!' because she had spotted a bird or flower that we 'just had to see.' My mother did this, too, and I have to admit that I am equally at fault—I earned the name Hawkeye from a friend for always spotting birds. We've taken the girls bird-watching, exploring waterfalls and tide pools, watching woodpeckers, climbing up rocks, chasing waves in the ocean, and admiring the Rockies. We've camped and hiked and wandered, and will continue to do so as a family."

The Outdoors

Being out in nature with your daughters is important. It's not just boys who like to climb, hike, and explore—so do daughters and moms, no matter their age. Patricia is a court-appointed public fiduciary, charged with managing the affairs of people who are incapacitated. She's always loved nature, and has made hiking a family tradition. "Until my mother became too frail, she and I would take walks whenever I visited. Those quiet times became a vehicle for her to share her fears about aging or concerns about loved ones. My daughter, Ceinwen, and I have continued this practice and schedule a hike whenever we visit each other. When we're out on the trail alone, we seem to open our hearts to each other more readily. We spend a lot of time talking about relationships, and she often seems to me to be older and wiser than I would expect from a woman of thirty years. Sometimes I feel as if I'm the daughter and she's the mother because of her insight. She talks to me about any problem she's having, whether it be with men or women friends, and we discuss possible ways of dealing with it. I can share my deepest feelings with her, as she can with me, without either of us judging the other."

Like Patricia, I am continually heartened by the loving bond I feel with my adult daughter. Spending time together away from noise and distractions has helped our friendship grow and deepen over the years. Heather and I usually go to the coast together for a few days each spring. We walk along the beach, talk long into the night about hopes and dreams, and reconnect, both with nature and with ourselves.

Those times together should start when a daughter is young, and Amy, in her mid-twenties, knows fresh air is not only good for your health, it's good for your soul. She and her two-year-old daughter, Liz, would rather be outside than in the house: "Even though it's only been around forty degrees, it's been sunny, so we bundle up and play outside until Liz wants to go back in. We love it! I never want to forget how nice it feels to have a strong wind and bright sunshine on my face. The sunshine seems to keep the 'terrible two's' away, and we both seem to be in a better mood when we come in from being outside. Liz eats more at lunchtime and takes a longer nap. We have two huge pecan trees in our backyard, and she loves to pick up pecans and pull off the outer hull. It's amazing how the small stuff makes life that much more enjoyable."

Native Traditions and Nature

Laurie is of Cherokee descent and has two daughters, nine and eleven. She is intent on teaching them about their heritage, including a very special way to view nature. "My children are still young, and I am teaching them certain skills and ways of looking at the world, and building their awareness step-by-step. For instance, in order to strengthen their interactions with wildlife, each time they bring creatures home we examine and watch them for a day or two, then let them go. I'm teaching my daughters that each species needs its own particular environment to survive, and I'm also hoping to cultivate their awareness of the importance of protecting natural habitats. My daughters are very conscious of nature, and through their curiosity and interaction with local animal and plant life, we have learned many lessons about how the earth provides and that we shouldn't interfere with natural animal instincts. My children are learning to honor the earth and leave the land unblemished. Through gardening, they have learned how to provide for the growth of plants naturally, how to tell when they're ready for harvesting, and how to prepare them for consumption.

"I believe in teaching them survival skills. They know how to build a good cooking fire, and have experienced many different meals cooked outdoors. I have also taught them how to make an oven out of a box wrapped in aluminum foil to bake things over coals, like potato casseroles, brownies, and many other recipes normally requiring a regular oven. They have learned how to purify water, identify animal tracks, find edible plants and berries, build a temporary shelter, read a compass, and judge time and direction based on the sun. My oldest daughter will have her first hunting experience this fall, and she has already watched me gut and skin a deer, as well as work the hide."

Wildcrafting

Laurie has been passing other Cherokee skills on to her daughters, too, including language, oral history, and traditions. We would term some of those lessons, including making rattles from gourds and fans from feathers found in the woods, wildcrafting (nature crafts or wild arts). For the Cherokee, these skills were a way of life. We can delve into the world of wildcrafting with our daughters by combining an exploration of nature with creativity.

Our ancestors learned that much of nature could be used for our benefit, but over time, those skills and traditions have been forgotten. The beauty of the natural world has also inspired artists and craftspeople throughout history. By looking closely at the possibilities nature offers, you will become more aware of the beauty around you. If you're walking along a stream, a closer look will show you rounded pebbles and stones, and green moss for collecting. If hiking in a forest, you'll notice pinecones, interesting grasses, and foliage to harvest; if at the beach, there'll be smooth gray driftwood battered by the sea to carry home. Wildcrafting takes the concept one step further with two key elements: collecting and creating. By harvesting directly from nature, we can create a variety of arts and crafts to please our senses and bring us into touch with the natural world.

Collection Displays

- Display pebbles or round rocks collected from a river, a stream, or the ocean in two or three clear jars of water in varying sizes. The water will emphasize the color and sheen of the rocks.
- Display small shells in glass bowls or use white glue to affix the shells to wooden boxes or wood-backed brushes or mirrors.
- Leaves and ferns are best displayed in simple or rustic frames. First, lay the leaves or ferns between two sheets of paper and press until dry under weight (a thick book will do). Next, disassemble a picture frame, lay the samples on the glass, add a backing sheet, and reassemble the frame. Adhesives are generally not necessary.

Herbs

Herbs have medicinal, culinary, and cosmetic properties, and are used throughout the world. In our country, much of the lore about native herbs has been forgotten but has recently become more popular as people seek a more nature-based way of living. Traditionally, herbalists have been women who passed their knowledge on to their daughters. Even if you're not interested in natural healing or cosmetics, you might be interested in reading about this old and ancient art and discussing it with your daughter. Some books that might be of help are: *The Way of Herbs: Fully Updated with the Latest Developments in Herbal Science,* by Michael Tierra; *The New Age Herbalist: How to Use Herbs for Healing, Nutrition, Body Care, and Relaxation,* by Richard Mabel and Michael McIntyre.

Flowers and Plant Life

Jeanne has involved her daughters in wildcrafting: "Our family has always been involved with nature. Mother and Grandma both took me to the woods to learn about the flowers, birds, and trees, and once I had my girls, I took them there as well. Grandma passed her love of flowers on to me and would let me come to garden club meetings with her. That's where I learned to make flowers out of seeds, corn cobs, seed pods, and such. My mom taught me how to make dolls out of hollyhock blooms, just as her mother had taught her. Of course, I taught my girls to make them, too. For a short while I worked for a florist, and although I taught the girls to make corsages and boutonnieres, they always preferred those little hollyhock dolls."

Any type of flowers, leaves, ferns, or wild grasses adds beauty and a touch of nature to any space. Wild grasses, gathered and tied with strands of raffia, can be striking in their simplicity—and easy to find growing in the country and along roadsides. The best time to harvest grasses is late in the growing season, when they have full heads of seed. Some will be quite dry already, while others should be spread flat in a warm, dry place for up to a week.

Another wonderful way to capture the beauty of the growing season throughout the year is to press flowers and leaves. Once dried, they can be glued in journals, used on handmade paper or notecards, or affixed to plain candles with a thin layer of melted wax using a small paintbrush. Here are some helpful hints:

- *Choose flowers that are fairly flat, like pansies or hydrangea blossoms, or remove the petals from multipetaled flowers, like roses, and press each one individually.*
- *Blot any moisture with a tissue, then lay the specimen on a piece of tissue paper. Lay another sheet of tissue paper on top and place this "sandwich" between the bottom pages of a heavy book.*
- *The flowers and leaves are ready when they feel dry and retain their shape when you lift them.*
- *Store carefully when dry, or leave in the book until ready to use.*

Drying flowers is another easy way to preserve their beauty. Some flowers are better suited to drying than others, and one way to test them is to touch them while they're still growing. Those with a natural dryness will generally preserve better than those that feel moist or dewy. Since flowers should be picked at mid-morning (after the dew has dried), you can easily combine a hike with a flower-picking excursion. Follow these steps for the best results:

- *Remove all the leaves from the stems (they don't dry well).*
- *Gather the stems into small bundles and secure with a rubber band.*

- *Hang upside down. One easy way is to attach two or three bunches (depending on size) to the bottom of a hanger with another rubber band or some string.*
- *Hang the hangers on hooks, in an open closet, or in any dry area that has plenty of circulation.*

PART FOUR

Style and Substance

Chapter 12

Life Appreciation

One way we learn to appreciate life is to experience all it has to offer—fine arts like music, theater, and dance; travel; sports; photography; literature; nature; and so much more. We can't hope to delve into all of these areas here, but we can certainly touch on a few. My friend Bobbi, who has both daughters and granddaughters, has been known to say, "Children are like computers. They need the right kind of 'input' because they will perform as programmed. Everything they see, hear, feel, and discover goes into what they become." I agree with Bobbi and think it makes sense to introduce our daughters to as many different aspects of life as possible so they can make informed decisions. How will they ever know if they like opera (or country western music, Picasso, birdwatching, science fiction, modern dance, or anything else) if they haven't experienced it?

I also think it's important that we start this education process early, because it's important to get past the "I can't" syndrome. Young children are generally open to new things and don't have a high fear of failure—or of doing something unusual, however you define that word. By the time a daughter enters her teenage years, she will have developed prejudices based on what her friends say and do, and what's popular in the media. The earlier you expose her to new experiences, the more comfortable she will be with the concept, as well as with trying new things later on in life.

Live Theater

The first time my mother took me and my sister to a play, I was only eleven, and my sister was thirteen. I don't remember the title of the play, but the main attraction was the actress Giselle MacKenzie. My mother was really looking forward to going, and my sister and I felt special because she'd invited us along. It was quite an exciting evening. The performance was held in a small theater-in-the-round, so even though I was short, I had a good view of the stage. I still remember the thrill of seeing an actress in person whom I'd seen on TV and thinking that television and the movies weren't nearly as exciting as live theater.

I took my daughter to her first live theater production for her thirteenth birthday. We went out for a fancy lunch, then to a matinee production of the musical *Annie.* She loved it. Later, I took her to see a musical drama, *The Barber of Seville.* I thought the play might be too dark, but she loved that one, too. Sometimes we tend to project our own tastes on what we think our daughters might or might not like. Instead, we need to keep an open mind and not limit their experiences to our own. Besides, we ourselves should continue to try new things as we grow older, and what better way to do that than invite our daughters along.

Jenn, a student, makes annual trips with her mother and sister to Stratford, in Ontario, Canada, for a Shakespeare festival. "I don't really remember how it started. My parents were both live theater aficionados, and from the time we were children, theater was part of family trips. But this is a special ritual—it's just the girls. Every year we stay in the same B&B and get the same room, one with a little second bedroom off it for me since my sleep habits are vastly different from those of my mother and sister. We try to see everything that's on at Stratford at the time, and we've been doing this long enough that we all have favorite actors and/or types of plays. We drive the surrounding country, shop for antiques, and eat. There's a chef school in Stratford, so the place is just full of incredible restaurants. I guess that's what the trip is really about for me—good food and wine, gorgeous plays, and an atmosphere that, no matter the stresses and tensions among us (and over the years there have been some), makes it possible for us to connect in ways we never dreamed of.

"Just recently my sister and I realized that we missed last year's outing because we were at opposite ends of the country. We talked about setting things up for this year, and our talk reminded me that rituals don't just *happen* but must be actively sought. I appreciate my mom for making all the arrangements year after year, but maybe now that my sister and I are older, it's time we took some responsibility for carrying on the tradition."

As Jenn has pointed out, traditions might be easy to start, but they're just as easy to end. Either way, all it takes is someone to remember—or forget. If there are traditions in your family that have gone by the wayside, why not get them going again? Some time, some thought, and a little work will surely get you back on track.

Dance

I took dance lessons when I was eight or nine, and discovered I loved tap and hated ballet. I remember loving the energy and sound of tap dance, and especially the fast-paced movements of certain steps that had names like Shuffling off to Buffalo. I also loved the colorful costumes, the bows on my tap shoes, and performing onstage (to the point where I might have been somewhat of a ham).

Phyllis has a daughter, Emily, and is enjoying carrying on the dance tradition her mother started with Phyllis and her sisters. "Aunt Jane had a dance studio, and Mother used to take me for ballet lessons. During class, Mom would sit in the back, and I could see her watching me and looking at me like I was a star. Now I know how she felt, because when I watch Emily perform, I can't help but think she is very talented, graceful, and cute. Everyone, including her teacher, tells me just how good she is and that she has a keen sense of music. After Aunt Jane, I advanced to another studio, where I'm sure I felt even more important. Perhaps I was never very talented, but my mother never let me think that."

Phyllis's memories are a clear illustration of how important it is for a daughter to have her mother's love and support. Looking back, Phyllis isn't so sure she was talented, but her mother certainly made her feel that way. My mother did the same. I remember how involved she was with my tap dancing. She made my costumes for recitals and was always there to watch me perform, taking the usual "proud parent" photographs and telling everyone I was the "best one onstage." Without her praise and encouragement, would I have practiced as much as I did? Would I have been able to walk onto that stage and dance my heart out? I don't know. But I do know that those memories are intertwined with warm, loving thoughts of my mother, which I often share with my daughter.

Culture

Most Americans have a heritage that began in another country. Whether that country is European, African, or located in any region of the world, our ancestry—and the focal point of *family*—provides an arena for mother and daughter to learn together about the traditions of their ancestors. Phyllis and her husband adopted Emily from China when she was a toddler, and they wanted her to learn about her native land's traditions and culture. "We put Emily in Chinese classes during the summer in order for her to learn the language, dances, and other traditions of her native country. We also keep in touch with the families that went to China with us to get Emily, and every year we have a reunion, even though they are all over the country. The girls have bonded and call themselves 'Chinese cousins.' " Emily might not be learning about Chinese customs and traditions firsthand, but her mother will bring them into her life, so they can be passed on to any daughters that Emily might have. You can start explaining your own culture to your daughter as well:

- *Stories and oral history passed down from parents and grandparents in your family should give you a good starting point for research.*
- *Read about the history and culture of your ancestors in sources at your library or on the Internet.*
- *Try narrowing your search and learn about language, dance, food, textiles, or some other part of your heritage that is of particular interest to you.*

Instrumental Music

In earlier times, music appreciation was part of most young women's education and training. However, that tradition is receiving much less attention today. Nevertheless, my family has a musical heritage that goes back several generations, and although my sister suffered a partial hearing loss, she still enjoyed music and took lessons in piano for a while. In grade school, I learned to play the flute, trumpet, and violin (because my grandfather played the fiddle), and finally settled on the piano. Although my mother had visions of my playing jazz, I chose classical music. After a few initial lessons showed I had some talent, my mother arranged for lessons from a retired concert pianist. I have clear, and very fond, memories of a studio with two grand pianos placed back to back, and playing for the sheer joy of how it made my heart soar. For a time, I harbored the dream of becoming a concert pianist. I even learned to play the jazz my mother enjoyed, dabbled in the blues, and tried my hand at writing rock-and-roll songs.

I carried on this musical tradition and encouraged my daughter to take advantage of lessons provided in school. She tried the violin (another example of a mother with preconceived notions), then settled on the clarinet, which she played throughout high school.

If your daughter's school doesn't provide lessons, you can still see that she has the opportunity to learn.

- *Check the yellow pages of your phone book for places that sell musical instruments. The store should also have a list of teachers and recommendations. If not, check through the classified ads of your local newspaper for group or private lessons. Be sure to accompany your daughter to the first lesson, so you can observe both the teaching and the learning.*
- *Don't let the cost of buying an instrument stop you. Many places will rent on a month-by-month basis (even if your daughter has her heart set on learning to play the piano), or you can buy used instruments in good condition at many pawnshops.*
- *If you have young children, you can always start small with a recorder, triangle cymbals, harmonica, maracas, digiridoo, tambourine, or any instrument that is small and easy to play.*

Singing

Lynnette has three daughters: Abigail, seven; Cecily (Bugs), four; and Anna, three. Lynnette discovered music as a child and learned to play the piano and Celtic whistle, took voice lessons, and sang in choirs and ensembles in school and church. "My mother and I share the love of singing. When she was a child, my mother would sit on her swing in the backyard and make up songs. She would sing them loudly and without hesitation. When I was growing up, I especially remember my mother singing in the morning. She usually sang silly little lyrics, but they brought joy to me and a cheerfulness to the household. I've decided that I want my children to have the same joy in their hearts in the morning, too, so first thing, I burst out to them singing:

"This is morning, with a song in my heart,
even when it's cloudy and gray.
This is morning, with a song in my heart
—every day's a beautiful day.

"They just roll their eyes and call me silly, but I know they love it. I also sing opera-style and dance around in my kitchen. They join in occasionally, calling me the 'kitchen dancer.' We live in the country, so I like to go outside and sing loudly and twirl around. My children really do think I'm nuts, but I just keep on, because I thought my mom was, too. Abigail has a love for music and has been singing practically since she was born. She is seven now, and I make sure to encourage her every time she sits down at the piano or sings. I don't want her to be insecure or shy about it, but to sing and play to her heart's content. I want the joy to overflow and affect those around her, and I want my grandchildren to have the same."

Reading

I have strong childhood memories of seeing my mother reading a book just about any time she wasn't doing something else. Following her example, my sister and I grew up loving to read. My mother didn't read us children's books—she read to us what *she* was reading, which was a bit of every genre—science fiction, multigenerational sagas, historical fiction, mysteries, and romance. Although you might think that was an unusual world of books for a child, I was exposed early on to all types of writing except literary fiction and nonfiction, which I tackled later.

My children grew up seeing me reading a lot. They also grew up being read to—I read them children's books of every sort, size, dimension, and subject. I took them to get their own library cards before they could read, and always let them take home as many books as they could carry. The library is a great place for children and adults to experience the wonder of reading. Check to see when your library has special events for children such as:

- *Story hours*
- *Summer read-a-book challenges*
- *Reading circles or groups*
- *Mother/daughter book clubs*

Jeanie combines her love of reading with music. She and her husband have a farm bed-and-breakfast where they host retreats and workshops. "We live in a very rustic setting, and one of our special times is in the evening, when we sit by the fireplace and read the C. S. Lewis Narnia series and *The Hobbit* and the Lord of the Rings trilogy aloud. When tucking Carrie in, I'd always sing three songs. The first was a nonsense song my mother sang, 'Green Bay Tree,' then 'Puff' and 'Hush-a-Bye.' I sat one evening here, before Carrie left for California, listening as she rocked her daughter, Summer, to sleep with the same songs. I'm thankful those songs aren't lost. One of the best and strongest gifts we have is the ability to give our children wings. We watch them experiment and grow stronger until finally they are strong enough in spirit to fly on their own."

Lynnette didn't know she loved to read until she was an adult, and now her family loves to read, too: "Something I've done with my children is read and then reread books they enjoy. This is fun for my children because they can begin to quote parts of the story and get involved with the characters. It causes conversations to go on during the day, too, especially when we are reading something like *Little House on the Prairie.* I am attempting to instill in my daughters a desire to read out loud in preparation for their motherhood years. I'm so very encouraged because Abigail loves to read to Cecily, her four-year-old sister, every night at bedtime. There is a sweet bond forming between them as sisters, and it is wonderful practice for future generations." Two books that will give you a great place to start this tradition are *100 Books for Girls to Grow On*, by Shireen Dodson, and *Great Books for Girls: More Than 600 Books to Inspire Today's Girls and Tomorrow's Women*, by Kathleen Odean.

There are so many books available, it's sometimes hard to choose which ones to read to your children. A good place to start is with books that have won awards. Listings should be available at your local library, bookstores, or on-line sources like www.amazon.com. Here are just a few awards for children's books:

- *The Newbery Medal, for the best children's book of the year; awarded by the Association for Library Service to Children*
- *Young Reader's Choice Award, awarded by the Pacific Northwest Library Association*
- *The Coretta Scott King Award, awarded by the American Library Association*

A few awards for books written for adult audiences are:

- *PEN/Faulkner Award (fiction)*
- *National Book Awards (fiction)*
- *Pulitzer Prize (six categories)*
- *The National Book Critics Circle Awards (five categories)*

Sports

A love of sports is definitely related to life appreciation. My daughter and I took tennis lessons through the Parks and Recreation Department of our city when she was in grade school. Our lessons were with different age groups, but we practiced together quite often. Ice-skating and gymnastics come to mind as other sports that are currently popular with young girls. Although gymnastics might be difficult to turn into a mother/daughter tradition, ice-skating is a great way to spend time with your daughter while getting in some good exercise.

Jeanne has two traditions in her family—soccer and the arts. "I started out as a player and soccer mom to Stephanie, then Melanie, and finally Torrey. At first, it was driving the game van full of girls whose parents couldn't come, helping with workouts, shagging balls, sewing on patches, and cooking spaghetti dinners. Then I wound up coaching for Torrey's team. We played on a women's team together, too—two years with Steph and one with Torrey. I started off teaching them all I knew and they went on to be better than I was."

Arts and Crafts

Jeanne's grandmother used to take Jeanne to the garden club with her: "We learned to make flowers out of dried seeds and such. She taught me to paint violets on blown-out eggs and how to do huck embroidery. My mother taught me to knit and bought me small loop looms to make potholders, my first easel, and tubes of paint. She and Grandma both took me to the woods to learn about the flowers, birds, and trees, and I, in turn, took the girls. When my girls were little, they accompanied me to art classes at the community school and drew or painted with me. They were my models for the French braiding classes that I taught, and I have their artwork framed and hung in several rooms of the house."

I think Jeanne makes an important point—it's important to exhibit your daughter's artwork. By displaying her work, you are also saying "I'm proud of you." That will encourage her to continue exploring and developing her talent. Here are just a few suggestions for displaying children's art:

- *Framed and hung in the living room, in the kitchen, or along a hallway that's designated "the artist's wall"*
- *In a large, bound scrapbook that's kept in a prominent place*
- *Affixed to the refrigerator with a magnet*
- *Pinned to a bulletin board in the computer room or den*

- *For pottery, ceramics, models, and other objects, display on bookshelves in any room of the house.*

Take a look at these suggestions, which may help you and your mother or daughter get involved in life-affirming activities:

- *If you live in a large city, take your daughter to an art museum. If you live in a small tourist area, visit art galleries. If neither attraction is available where you live, go to the library and find books that focus on individual artists or movements. Learning together can be fun.*
- *Look into dance or movement classes (yoga or stretching, for example) to take with your teenage or adult daughter.*
- *Ask your child (any age) if she'd like to go to a play, the ballet, or a musical performance.*
- *Start a mother/daughter reading group with women you know or with the mothers of your daughter's friends.*

Chapter 18

Entitaining

When most of us look back on childhood memories of parties, holidays, and entertaining, our thoughts turn immediately to our mothers. Traditionally, moms plan and organize social functions, whether they do everything themselves, hire a caterer, or include you, your sisters, and your brothers in both the work and the fun of the occasion. Many mothers fill the role of gracious hostess, making guests feel welcome and comfortable, whether they're entertaining at home or holding court at restaurants or lavish, catered affairs. That's quite a lot for one woman to do, and those skills aren't generally taught in any schoolroom. We either learn from our mothers or we figure it out on our own through trial and error. In this, as in most cases, I think it's better to have Mom as a teacher, rather than learning the hard way.

Childhood memories also shed light on how and why we develop our own way of entertaining. If your mother invited people to your home quite often, you probably see entertaining as part of the ritual of daily life or as a way to spice up a weekend. If she did all the planning, cooking, and cleaning up, you might think entertaining at home is a lot of work. Did your mother set a formal table, elaborately decorated with silver, china, and flowers, or did she prefer casual buffets where the guests helped themselves? She may have done both—or neither. In the best of worlds, life should be a balance, and that includes entertaining. Whether you prefer formal dinner parties or casual get-togethers, cocktail parties, a weekend brunch, or afternoon tea, entertaining, especially at home, gives you an opportunity to teach your daughter the art of being gracious, as well as the skill of creating a warm, inviting atmosphere.

Creative Entertaining

Kristin remembers her mother's natural talent for elegance and her special knack for coming up with unusual ideas. When Kristin lived in San Diego, her mother was known for her "shrimp parties." "I remember my sister and I going to the ocean side of Point Loma, carrying gallon-sized glass pickle jars each with a bail handle and good lid. Then we'd wade out about waist deep until the seawater was clear and no longer carrying sand, and fill the jars with seawater to take back home. Mom would cook pounds and pounds of shrimp in that perfectly salted seawater and drain them well. Then she would put three or four very tall, slim brass candlesticks on a huge oval tray and cover the tray and several inches of the candlesticks with foil. The rest of the dinner was a wonderful leafy salad, some crusty bread, and individual bowls of flavored melted butter for dipping. We set out lots of napkins and placed the tray, piled high with shrimp, with the candles lit, in the center of the table."

Kristin's mother extended that spark of creativity to children's parties, too. When Kristin was in the Brownies and Girl Scouts—and, of course, at her birthday parties—her mother had a unique way of serving drinks: "She put a drop of food coloring in drinking glasses, then added a couple of ice cubes to 'hide' the food coloring. Then, on the patio or in the dining room, she would serve her 'magic drinks,' and with curious girls watching, she'd pour 7-Up into the glasses. Magically, some glasses filled up with pink bubbles, others with yellow, green, or blue. My friends always thought my mother's 'magic drinks' were very mysterious."

A Family Affair

Recently, Cindy's daughter, seven, and son, ten, entertained their grandparents as part of their homeschool curriculum and a book they'd studied about a boy whose father ran a pizzeria. "The week's project was to create a pizza restaurant and invite their grandparents to dinner. The kids created their own menu, made the pizza crust and sauce from scratch, and made an antipasto platter, fresh salad, garlic breadsticks, and three kinds of pizza. Our dining room was transformed with a banner that read JOHNSON'S PIZZERIA. The kids wore white aprons and treated their grandparents as if they were really special customers in their restaurant. I was so proud of them that night, seeing my mom's influence spreading through the generations as they practiced hospitality through entertaining."

Special anniversaries are usually a time of celebration, and Amy remembers that the biggest party her mom ever gave was for her grandparents' fiftieth wedding anniversary. "Even though the party itself was only one day, we had cousins and relatives in from all over the country, and it seemed to go on forever. I was in third grade, and an entire week seemed like forever to me. Mom let us stay home from school, but every day we all had to sit at the kitchen table to do our homework. With seven children in my family and our six cousins from Massachusetts, it was almost like a one-room schoolhouse. That party was also my first memory of wearing a really fancy dress. It was pink, floor length, and trimmed in lace and flowers. I thought I was so grown up. Grandma and Grandpa have passed their sixtieth anniversary and are both in their nineties now, but each time I go back to Chicago to visit them, I always drive past the banquet hall and remember that special celebration. I hope to help plan for my parents' fiftieth anniversary, and with my seven siblings, their spouses and children, I can only imagine that my daughter will remember such a celebration exactly as I do—fondly."

An English Ritual

If you haven't experienced a typical English tea party, you're missing an experience. The stage will be set with an antique silver tea service, fragile china, tiered crystal serving dishes holding tiny sandwiches with the crusts cut off, and cakes and shortbread served with rich, clotted cream from Devon. Since tea is traditionally served between three and four o'clock in the afternoon, dinner is obviously served quite late. Entertaining with a British tea might be a bit elaborate, but you can pull it off, and your guests will certainly be impressed. Serving afternoon tea to three or four of your women friends can be an especially gracious way to entertain.

When Carol visited England after college, she fell in love with serving tea and created an Americanized version to share with friends. "I have a lovely patio and garden, but don't like to barbecue, I started having my own afternoon tea outdoors during spring and summer, and over the years invited a few of my friends to join me. Once Jennie was ten or eleven, she started joining us, and now we have several mother/daughter teas while school's out. We have one table for the girls and another

Tea Menu

A selection of finger sandwiches (such as cucumber, tomato and cheese, or deviled egg)
Scones with preserves
Traditional trifle with lady fingers
Miniature pastries, cake, or homemade cookies
and
Strong English tea (such as Earl Grey)

Cucumber and Cream Cheese Finger Sandwiches

12 ounces softened cream cheese
½ small onion, grated
2 to 3 tablespoons mayonnaise
Sliced wheat bread
2 medium cucumbers, peeled, seeded, and sliced thinly

Combine the cream cheese and onion. Add mayonnaise a tablespoon at a time until the mixture is spreadable. Cut the crusts off a slice of bread and spread with the mixture. Top with sliced cucumbers and another piece of bread. Cut diagonally twice to create triangles. Makes 20 to 30 finger sandwiches.

How to Brew a Pot of Tea

1. Fill a kettle with water (enough for however many cups of tea you want plus one cup) and heat until just boiling.
2. Pour a little of the boiling water into the teapot, swirl it around to heat the pot, then discard.
3. For each cup of tea, add 1 tablespoon tea leaves (or, if you must, 1 tea bag) directly into the warmed pot, or use a mesh tea ball.
4. Pour hot water into the teapot and let steep for 4 to 5 minutes.
5. Before pouring tea, offer guests milk, sugar, or honey and lemon slices. (The British traditionally add milk to the cup *before* pouring the tea.)
6. Pour the tea (using a tea filter to strain out the tea leaves) into cups.
7. Keep the pot covered with a cozy to keep the tea warm.

for moms, so Jennie gets to decide how to decorate 'her' table and which cups and saucers to use. I have good china, but decided to buy some secondhand cups and saucers so Jennie could set her table without me worrying about breakage. We use tablecloths and napkins, serve two kinds of tea (whichever new ones we want to try, or our favorite English breakfast tea), traditional tiny sandwiches of watercress or cucumber and cream cheese, and plates of luscious desserts. Jennie and I enjoy planning our little tea parties, and it's a wonderful way to get to know her friends and their moms."

Part of the Team

When Deborah was growing up, her mother didn't entertain often, but she did take the time to teach Deborah and her brothers how to entertain properly. "First, we tidied up the whole apartment, then we helped Mum in the kitchen with chopping and stirring. Extra care was taken in setting the table, and my brothers and I put snacks and cold items out before the guests arrived. If it was a party that involved friends and relations, we acted as mini hosts by taking coats and wraps, and putting them on my parents' bed, then offered drinks and snacks on trays. I remember a particular party, for which Mum had made a French onion soup. The soup was delicious and going fast, but for some strange reason we never actually ran out of soup. When Mum and I compared notes after the party, we realized that my mother, my older brother, and I had all been adding water and soup cubes every so often to keep from running out. After having a good laugh, we decided the soup had seemed to improve as the evening went on.

"Parties at home were definitely an extended-family affair, and we were all involved (grandparents, children, and grandchildren)—working in the kitchen, cooking; in the dining room, making sure that bowls of food were kept full; and in the living room, passing out finger food. Mum remembers helping her mom prepare for parties when she was a kid because her parents entertained a lot. One of the main things I was taught, and am now teaching my daughter, is to greet guests at the door when they arrive and to see them to the door when they leave. Well, the tradition goes on, because when we entertain the kids are expected to help in the preparations, tidy up the house, set out dinnerware, and do odd jobs in the kitchen. They've also started putting coats upstairs when guests arrive and bringing them down when they leave. Sarah particularly loves to be of real help. I'm amazed at how much I do with her without thinking when, in fact, it is a tradition I learned at home. Now I'm passing it along."

Real Entertainment!

Jeanette's daughter, Abigail, is only nine, but she loves to write, produce, and direct plays for their guests. "Abigail usually picks a seasonal theme, and invites her younger brothers and cousins to be in the play, too. They rehearse their parts, choose costumes from our costume trunk, and Abigail writes up invitations and tickets to the event. Believe me, our guests are usually in for quite a treat. We also have the children memorize lines from famous plays, stories, and poems, and they are always ready to recite for guests. Abigail loves to entertain and usually rises to the occasion by enhancing her recitation with dance and costumes."

The Audience

If you send your children to bed when you entertain at home, remember that just because they're in bed, they aren't necessarily asleep. Jeannette has childhood memories of eavesdropping with her sister: "When I was a child, we weren't allowed to stay up when Mom and Dad had parties at our house. My older sister and I did not like that at all, so when the party was in full swing, we would sneak out of bed, crouch quietly at the top of the stairs, and listen to all the adults talking. It was great fun, and we often had to stifle our own laughter at the funny things that were said. Our parents were Dutch immigrants, as were many of their friends, and they would mix English and Dutch in their wonderful hearty conversations. In the morning, we had to be careful not to give ourselves away by repeating what we had heard at the top of the stairs."

Setting a Lovely Table

Just because you have children doesn't mean you can't set a lovely table, complete with china, silver, and linen. After all, you'll want your daughter to learn how to set the mood and tone of a wonderful evening for her own friends and family someday. Creative centerpieces and napkins, and the design of their fold, can add interest to any table.

Lee Ann, a photographer, remembers that her mother entertained at home quite often: "When Mother was planning a dinner party, my sister and I always helped polish the silver. It might seem odd, but we always looked forward to this job. Mom wanted the silver polished the week before whatever party or celebration we were having, so she wasn't in a hurry. Most of her silver had been passed down through the family, and as we polished each piece, Mom would reminisce about the family member it belonged to, her memories of celebrations and holidays when she was little, how the teapot got its dent, and other stories. Then she'd start in on tales about different relatives. My sister and I used to call those tales silver stories, and we loved for her to tell them over and over. Now that Mom has given me some of those silver pieces, I feel like the relatives from generations past are sitting down at the table with me. My daughter is only four, but in a few years I'll have her help me polish the silver and listen to my silver stories."

> ### Centerpiece
>
> Vases
> 16 to 32 ounces fresh
>   cranberries
> 2 or 3 limes, sliced
> Small votive candles
>
> Arrange 3 to 5 clear cylindrical vases of different heights on a mirror or a silver tray. Make sure the vases are larger in circumference than the limes. Fill the vases with alternating layers of cranberries and slices of lime. Fill with water and float a small candle on top of each vase. The fruit will look fresh for at least a week, then discard.

It's a good idea to use lists when entertaining to save headaches, stress, and the "Oops!" mistakes we *all* want to forget. Depending on the age of your daughter, use this opportunity to teach her the basics of Entertaining 101. Here are some tips on devising a minimalist "to do" list:

- *Choose a date, compile a list of guests, and clear the date with important invitees. If sending written invitations, mail them at least two weeks prior to the event.*
- *List the cleaning tasks needed, when they should be completed, and arrange for any outside services.*

- *Decide whether you want an overall theme, mood, or color scheme, and if you want to do any decorating (candles, centerpieces, or special lighting, for example).*
- *Prepare a menu, considering any special meal requirements (vegetarian, nondairy, or sugar-free or low-fat, for example), list all the ingredients you need (in generous proportions), and write down where you can find them.*
- *If you decide to enlist professional help (bartender, florist, caterer for special dishes such as desserts or canapés), make arrangements two or three weeks ahead of time.*
- *Shop early to ensure that you can find everything you need (including fresh or potted flowers for the table, votive candles, and other items) and to alleviate last-minute stress.*
- *List personal preparations ("dress to dry cleaner," for example) and timetable, and schedule any appointments (hairdresser or rug shampooer, for example).*

Chapter 14

Caring and Compassion

*H*aving compassion for families, friends, and those in need is a tradition women have honored throughout history. Giving of ourselves is both the heart and the soul of women, and has been a tradition of feminine culture for centuries. Caring about others also brings out the best we have to offer. We are the givers of life—if not always biologically, then in assuming the primary role in caring for the emotional well-being of our families. It seems that we nurture instinctively more so than men and, by example, pass this attribute on to our daughters.

Most of us have never been homeless, hungry, or destitute, but we might have found ourselves very much in need at some time in our lives. That time came for me when my daughter and I were the victims of a drunk driver. The accident was bad, the repercussions serious. Heather and I were both hurt, and my injuries were fairly severe. I was hospitalized for a week, and out of work for almost five months. I was a single mom with no family nearby to help, and felt vulnerable and completely overwhelmed. People say the worst times can bring out the best in people, and I found that to be true. My situation may have been dire, but it wasn't long before things changed for the better.

The accident happened on the night before Thanksgiving, a time when people are busy and looking forward to family celebrations. Nevertheless, my friends stepped in and took care of things. My sister whisked my son, Brian, who wasn't in the accident, off to Disneyland for three days, then cared for him while I was in the hospital. When Heather was released after a few days, my friend

Get-Well Basket

A good novel or crossword
  puzzle book
A thermos of hot chicken soup
An inexpensive mug filled with
  herbal tea bags
A small bouquet or plant
A box of tissues
Cough drops
A get-well card

Joie's family welcomed her into their home with love and reassurance. A neighbor fed my cats, watered my plants, picked up the mail, and kept an eye on things.

When I finally came home from the hospital, I worried over how I would take care of myself, let alone my children. Carolyn, a friend from work, organized a "supper brigade" at the office. Friends—and some women I hardly knew—signed up to make dinner for me and the kids for an entire month. Carolyn delivered casseroles on her way home from work every night, cheered me up, and kept me up-to-date on the office. My employers graciously kept my paychecks coming, and Carolyn even did my banking.

Years later, I reminded her just how much she'd helped me during that time, but Carolyn insisted her good deeds were "no trouble at all." She taught me something she already knew well—that food, conversation, and a helping hand give people in need a sense of community and caring. Carolyn's daughter, Adele, learned that lesson early on. She grew up helping her mother prepare hot meals for people who were ill, in mourning, or going through bad times. Adele carries on this tradition, much as her mother did, by including her daughter in volunteer projects at church and in the community.

If you know of a sick friend or neighbor, fill a pretty basket with things that will make him or her feel better and bring a little sunshine into his or her day. You can easily customize the basket for any age.

When mothers carry out selfless acts and include their daughters (no matter their age), the shared satisfaction of helping others is directed both introspectively and into the relationship. Knowing you can count on each other definitely strengthens the bond between mother and daughter. When people helped me, my anxiety lifted. I felt that the chaos we'd been thrown into was somehow under control, that I was loved and cared for, and that my children would be all right. Words could not convey my thanks and appreciation.

If you'd like to offer kindness to someone, keep your eyes and ears open to discover just the right opportunity. Better yet, make a few phone calls and volunteer. Have a list of days and hours you're available, what you're able to do, and what training, if any, you might have. You should check your phone book under "Social Service Agencies" for a comprehensive list, but here are a few possibilities:

- *Red Cross*
- *Salvation Army*
- *Churches or synagogues*
- *Hospitals*
- *Soup kitchens*
- *Food banks*
- *Nursing homes*

If you have young children, ask if they can accompany you. Although that won't be possible in a hospital, it probably would be in a nursing home or soup kitchen. You also don't have to be part of a formal volunteer program or wait for an emergency—whether you have a friend who's working long hours or the woman you see every day

Quick Banana Nut Bread

1 cup sugar
½ cup vegetable shortening
2 eggs
1 cup mashed ripe bananas
1 teaspoon lemon juice
2 cups sifted flour
3 teaspoons baking powder
½ teaspoon salt
1 cup chopped nuts

Cream sugar and shortening together. Beat eggs until light, and add. Press bananas through sieve (or mash with a fork), and add lemon juice. Blend with creamed mixture. Sift flour, baking powder, and salt together and mix into banana mixture. Add nuts and bake in buttered loaf pan in preheated 325° oven for 1 hour or until toothpick inserted in bread comes out clean.

in the elevator has fractured her arm, delivering a home-cooked meal will definitely make a person in need feel better.

For a wonderful, nourishing breakfast, make banana nut bread, add a bowl of strawberries (washed and trimmed), a thermos of hot coffee or cocoa, and a get-well card.

For a comfort food for lunch or dinner, ask your mother for her famous chicken soup recipe. Whatever you decide, remember to choose a dish that is easy to transport and that reheats well.

It does seem as though traditions started in childhood have lasting effects on the way women see the world and their role within their communities. By helping people, children learn kindness, compassion, patience, and respect for others. Volunteering as a family is also a great way to spend time together on a project that has meaning for all of you. Consider this:

- *Saturdays and Sundays are good days to join environmentalists to clean ocean beaches or help in a community effort to fix up a children's playground.*
- *If you have a car, you and your daughter could deliver meals to shut-ins and the elderly through an organization like Meals-on-Wheels.*
- *A few hours in the evening is a good time to work at a homeless shelter that serves teens or the disenfranchised, a nursing home, or with the handicapped.*
- *For a less-structured project, you and*

Rosemary Chicken

6 chicken thighs or 3 split
   breasts
¼ cup flour
3 or 4 cloves garlic
Olive oil
8 small red potatoes
1 large onion
6 medium carrots
1 cup chicken stock
2 sprigs rosemary
Salt and pepper

Lightly dust chicken pieces with flour, then brown chicken and garlic (minced or crushed) in a lightly oiled pan. Place in baking dish. Quarter potatoes and onion, slice carrots, and add. Pour chicken stock over the chicken. Add rosemary, and salt and pepper to taste. Cook in preheated 350° oven for 45 minutes, then let cool. (When delivering this dish, write a note with instructions to reheat in a 350° oven for 30 minutes.)

your mother can collect food, clothing, and blankets for the needy.

- *If you want to include small children, I suggest you contact service organizations and find one prepared and happy to work with kids. Also, be sure to ask about project and job descriptions, as well as any safety issues.*

Be a realist when assessing your own interests, skills, and commitment in conjunction with any program you're considering. Mentoring a disadvantaged student might appeal to you, but it also requires a long-term commitment. Decide whether a "drop-in" program might be easier to start with. Groups that prepare meals for the homeless, food banks, and groups with ongoing organized activities are usually happy to see an extra pair of hands any day of the week.

If you're wondering how to figure out what your community needs, you might start with the places and people who come into contact with people in need. Here are just a few:

- *Community action and environmental groups*
- *Hospitals*
- *Social service agencies*
- *Nursing homes*
- *Assisted-living facilities*
- *Special programs for the handicapped or disadvantaged*
- *Mentoring and literacy programs*
- *Big Brothers and Big Sisters*
- *After-school programs in sports or the arts*
- *Providers of meals for homeless people*

Patti, a volunteer master gardener, knew she wanted to instill a sense of service in her daughters, but she also wanted the experience to be fun. When Marcy, Misty, and Mercy were three, five, and nine, respectively, Patti transformed Halloween forever. Patti wanted the girls to learn about giving rather than "gimme." She decided to have the girls dress up for Halloween and visit a nursing home. "Since Halloween is traditionally a children's holiday, parents normally take their children around to collect goodies, and the home's residents don't expect company. They were thrilled with our visit, and there was a lot of happiness shared on both sides as our girls gave out candy to the residents. We visited for many years, enjoying the lovely blind lady who 'saw' my daughters' faces and costumes with her hands, and the wily little man in the wheelchair who chased the girls up and down the halls for more candy and laughed so happily you had to join him."

As the girls grew older, Patti came up with another way to combine volunteerism with Halloween: "We worked on a Halloween 'safe house' our church had set up for the neighborhood children. This was a safe alternative to trick-or-treating, and has become an annual event. We decorated the church with all the sights of autumn, including scarecrows, pumpkins, and cornstalks, and served hot dogs, cider, and popcorn. Adults and older children set up and supervised the booths for playing games and winning candy prizes, an artist volunteered his time to make caricatures of the children, and clowns made balloon animals. All the excitement of a day at the fair was shared with the children, and at the end of the evening each got a bag of candy to take home."

Marcy is now a mother herself, and intends to pass on the tradition of volunteerism to both her son and her daughter. Her mother served as an example to her daughters and taught them that people should think of others less fortunate than themselves. Marcy, Misty, and Mercy will always remember their mother as compassionate and selfless. That gift that will last through their lifetimes and beyond, as they teach their own children the spirit of giving.

Holidays are a perfect time to start new traditions—or turn old traditions into something truly special. They are times when families come together, and they are the times we tend to remember. If you'd like to make a tradition of volunteerism on holidays throughout the year, here are a few suggestions:

- *Veterans Day—accompany an elderly military widow to a local parade, or invite her to church or dinner.*
- *Independence Day—volunteer to record books-on-tape for the blind.*
- *Presidents Day—volunteer in a literacy program and teach people to read.*
- *Thanksgiving—serve dinner to the homeless or deliver food boxes to the needy.*
- *Christmas—help make gift baskets with your church or the Salvation Army, or visit a nursing home.*

Ellen learned about helping others by watching her mother start the gift shop in their synagogue, remembering birthdays and special occasions, and sharing food, magazines and her famous hand-knit slippers with everyone she knew. Her lessons took hold when Ellen started volunteering when she was six, making and selling pot holders to raise money for the Red Cross: "Mom always gave me lovely ideas about things I could do for others. When I was a teenager, I volunteered at the hospital, during college I staffed a health hot line, and later I taught others to read in a literacy project." Ellen's mother gave her the opportunity to experience life on a bigger scale, to develop compassion, understanding, patience, and a deep appreciation for all that she has.

Many women volunteer in their communities at shelters, hospitals, churches, schools, or with the needy and underprivileged. Some go one big step further and make volunteering a family tradition. I met Sharon when I was a teenager, and we've been friends ever since. Her mother, Betty, cares about people and shows it in a big way. Over the years, Betty has donated her time and love to the homeless, to battered women, and to her church and community. The city of Scottsdale, Arizona, recently honored Betty's outstanding volunteer work and commitment by awarding her the Frances Young Community Hero Award.

Sharon volunteers alongside her mother, delivering clothes and food to needy families and helping out wherever she's needed. Thanksgiving has always been a special day for Sharon's family—for years, they've helped cook and serve Thanksgiving dinner at a homeless shelter. Sharon's daughter Mary volunteers and teaches at her church, and her daughter Sherry has served as a foster mother and is an ardent advocate for the homeless.

Fran, a novelist, learned strength and fortitude from her mother, who faced hard times and tragedy during her life. Fran's grandmother was ill through the latter half of 1933 and 1934, and Fran's mother nursed her, cooked supper after school, and cleaned house on the weekends. This was during the Great Depression, and the family had little money for extras. What amazes Fran the most is that when her mother describes those times, she doesn't complain or think too much was asked of her. She talks mostly about how much she loved her mother and that her mother was always smiling and cheerful.

Fran's mother is now confined to a wheelchair and lives in a nursing home. Never complaining, Fran has followed her mother's example by keeping an eye on those who are bedridden or suffering from Alzheimer's. Fran sees her mother every day and takes her for long car rides on weekends. "Looking back, I realize how lucky I've been to have this remarkable woman for a mother. She's always been there for me—from my first love, the birth of my children, the death of my oldest son, to the sale of my first book. My mother will never walk again, but I stand in awe of her." Fran is part of the third generation of women in her family to pass on strength of character, caring, and compassion, although her inheritance reaches much farther back in time.

My own brush with adversity, and the selflessness of those who helped me, made a big impact in my life. I can never repay their kindness, but I can volunteer my time to help others. Over the years, I've been active in causes of mental and emotional health, the homeless, and people in crisis. There's an old truism that I've come to live by—you can't pay back, but you *can* pay forward. If you've been the recipient of kind acts, be sure to pass those good deeds on to someone else. Here are a few ideas to help make volunteerism a tradition in your family:

- *Arrange to visit a nursing home, and take your children with you. If your children don't have grandparents nearby, "adopt" an older person. I don't mean legally, but you <u>can</u> forge a bond with elderly people that serves both them <u>and</u> you. You and your children can write letters, visit, take them on short outings, to church or synagogue, and let them into your life while showing an interest in theirs. This could be especially meaningful if your parents live far away or have passed on.*
- *If you knit or crochet, make soft, lightweight caps for cancer patients. Deliver them personally to patients in the hospital—and take the kids with you. If your daughter or mother doesn't know how to knit or crochet, teach her.*
- *Contact a charitable organization that aids handicapped children, and organize a sporting event. Local schools or recreational parks might have facilities and equipment you can use. You will have expenses, and since this is for charity, you can also solicit donations from local businesses.*
- *Mentor a child at a local school. If you have an older daughter who does well in school, you could tutor grade school children together.*
- *Organize a visit by children in kindergarten to a rest home. Bring crayons, colored pencils, and paper so the kids and the residents can do artwork together.*
- *Bake cookies with your daughter and deliver them to neighbors.*
- *If you have an elderly or handicapped neighbor, team up with your teen and volunteer to mow the yard and trim shrubbery. If this person lives in an apartment complex, offer to wash the windows or floors.*
- *Volunteer to teach low-income families a variety of life*

skills—personal and family management, parenting, nutrition and food safety, employment skills, resource management, and community building. See if your state university extension office offers classes that will enable you to become certified as a volunteer life skills instructor, as I did.

Chapter 15

Spirituality

*S*pirituality means different things to different people. It can imply belief in a particular religion or doctrine, or reverence for God or a universal spirit. To some, God is a life force; to others, he/she is a personal god who rewards or punishes people for their actions. Spirituality can also allude to the mysterious depths of the human soul, or speak to moral values, love, or affinity with the natural world. In all cases, spirituality implies devotion, respect, and an acknowledgment of something sacred. A strong spiritual base can bring us closer to one another, help us achieve a more balanced life, and provide a meaning beyond our *selves*. These beliefs are especially important for mothers to explore with the daughters who will take them into the next generation.

At a time when many are in despair, there are those who reaffirm a return to our religious roots and a growing search for self-awareness. For those seeking spiritual fulfillment, there are many guides: mainstream religions, New Age concepts, paganism, a more global focus on Islam and Eastern religions (especially Buddhism), authors who have a thoughtful and relevant voice, and memoirs focused on a spiritual or monastic path of contemplation and a quiet faith. Spirituality can be expressed in many ways by many different people, and similar beliefs co-exist in many forms.

This country was colonized by people who feared God, believed in old faiths and religions, and held staunch Puritan values. Little did they know their search for religious freedom would succor generations of truth-seekers embracing a range of themes from formalized religion to a holistic approach to health and ecology, goddess worship, reincarnation, the supernatural, astrology, mysticism, and others. This range of religious diversity is an American tradition and will surely continue as long as we are seekers who wish to explore the spiritual dimension of our lives. As our daughters grow, question, and learn, they may choose different spiritual paths than their mothers did. Although this might be difficult for the mothers, I think we need to encourage self-awareness in all its expressions, including spirituality.

Children's Services

I have fond memories of going to Sunday school when I was a child, although I remember more about wearing pretty dresses and shiny new shoes than lessons about Jesus. Maybe because Bible school comprised two full weeks instead of an hour a week, I remember more about those summer sessions. I remember reading the Bible, for both the stories and the lessons, and the teacher leading discussions about how we could apply those lessons to our young lives. We did arts and crafts, and put on a short play for our parents on the last day of Bible school. Overall, I came away feeling reassured about my place in a community with lessons and beliefs that even a seven-year-old could understand. Churches, temples, synagogues, and other spirituality-based organizations offer structure and a sense of belonging, a common yearning among people of any age or belief, and certainly among girls and young women.

When I was fourteen, we moved from Arizona to Los Angeles and into an apartment complex located across the street from a church. We were Christians, but not active in a particular denomination, so one church served as well as another. My sixteen-year-old sister and I went to a church service and were invited to attend a youth group meeting later that night. Everyone was friendly and inviting, so we went. We met a number of great kids within the arms of a philosophical framework that encouraged faith, strength, and good morals. I think that's pretty good place for young girls to be.

If you have daughters that aren't part of a faith-based organization, consider taking a step in that direction. Most churches and synagogues have an open house once a month, when new people are made to feel especially welcome. You might also inquire about youth services or groups.

Judaism

Ellen, a psychologist, attended temple as a child but drifted away after she left home to attend college. "I knew there was something missing in my life, but it wasn't until after my daughters were born that I returned to my faith. I remember one service in particular, when the rabbi talked about how the old laws and customs mean as much today as they did when they were first written, and that it was important to bring our children to God. I connected with an inner calling that day, and decided that Diana and Rachel would grow up in a spiritual home. To prepare for her Bat Mitzvah last year, Diana studied Hebrew and the Torah. Rachel will start her studies soon, and recently asked me about the Torah. I was so glad to have that discussion with her. I told her the Torah isn't a set of laws, but a framework for thinking about things on many different levels, and no matter how many levels we discover, there are still more to come. It also gives meaning to our lives and asks us to live according to a high spiritual standard. I'm raising my girls to believe in God and to follow the teachings of their faith. With a strong foundation, I hope the rest of their lives will fall into place."

Religiously Mixed Marriages

Fran, a novelist, has strong memories of religious issues that surrounded her mother and father, and helped shape her own history. "Differences in religion were a very real issue for my mother's generation. For Roman Catholics, especially, ecumenism was an unknown. Outside the 'one true church' lay only purgatory and damnation. My mother had not yet converted when she married my father, and she had to agree to raise any children from their union as Catholic. After their wedding in a priest's parlor, she decided to take instructions in the church. None of my grandparents attended my parents' wedding, mainly because both my parents were marrying 'out of their faith.' My mother never bemoaned the fact that they didn't come to the wedding, but I know it must have hurt her deeply. In some ways, my mother was a better Catholic than my father, not at all uncommon for converts.

"Despite the fact that my mother now lives in a nursing center, she still receives Holy Communion every Sunday and finds solace in her religion. But when I was young, and my sister, brother, and I worried aloud about our Protestant friends and neighbors' going to hell when they died, Mom always said, 'We all worship the same God, and if people are good on earth, God will welcome them into heaven right along with the Catholics.' I think my mother's tolerant attitude toward everyone she met was a good example for her children. She taught us to judge people on the basis of their behavior, not on their religion, race, or ethnicity. And my mother's lessons will live on for generations, as my brother, sister, and I pass them on to our children."

When parents of different faiths have children, the issue of spirituality can be difficult and confusing, especially for the children. Deborah is Jewish; her husband is Episcopalian. "The kids know that there are differences between Bill's and my backgrounds, and they are also aware that I am somewhat uncomfortable with some of the Jesus stories. I've been candid with them that the reason I'm uncomfortable is that I was brought up believing certain things, but that I try to keep an open mind. And we always tell them that different people feel and think differently about things. We feel that celebrating the various holidays is important, but we try to keep them simple and closer to the original meaning in some sense.

"What we're trying to do is raise our children with some spirituality in their daily lives. For instance, they know that when I spin or weave, I don't get flustered about little inconsistencies or mistakes. We are all human, and I see mistakes as a reminder that none of us is perfect. We've explained that we believe there's an entity we call God who is the closest thing possible to perfect and has many different interpretations, depending on each person and culture. We've also told them that we feel whether or not you go to a house of worship, the most important thing is to try your best to be good. Instead of formal instruction, it's been more of a matter of answering questions that come up naturally. We also see holiday celebrations more as a matter of tradition and a way to celebrate our heritage, rather than our religion. Whenever we celebrate a holiday, we always spend time with the kids explaining its historical or religious significance."

Nature-Based Spirituality

Laurie, of Cherokee descent, has two young daughters. She is introducing them to the spiritual aspects of the Red Road, a term used by Native Americans to describe the path each person travels during her or his lifetime on Mother Earth. "We have many talks about how Spirit is in everything. My oldest daughter understands this concept very well. She came home from school recently very offended by one of her teacher's comments about her belief that Spirit is even in rocks. The teacher said, 'Well, it's a good thing we don't believe that anymore!' That's just not true. My daughters are learning to honor all of Creation with respect, that the plants and animals have life just as we do, to give thanks for all that is provided, and to take no more than we need. I see this belief system as a natural extension of their childlike wonder with the world. Their play reflects that they know deep down that all of the earth's creatures are connected and that all are an important part of the whole."

Many people are coming full circle and returning to the spiritual ways of people who live close to nature. Connect with yourself and the wonderful creatures of the earth—trees, water, plants, rocks, and animals. People who espouse a nature-based spirituality believe that being attuned to the natural world will help bring knowledge, balance, and harmony to everyone—and everything—on the planet. If you're interested in exploring this concept, you first need to experience the natural world. Not structured parks, landscaped gardens, zoos, or wildlife exhibits, but nature preserves, bird sanctuaries, forests of old-growth trees, estuaries, grasslands, desert wilderness, and snowcapped mountains. Travel outside civilization to explore the many facets of nature, and you may also discover a connective spirit.

The Bible

Michelle is general manager for a wholesale distributor, and is surprised that her six-year-old daughter already loves to read the Bible. "Katie seems to have a stronger link to God and spirituality than I had at her age. Her Bible goes everywhere with her, especially in the car. As soon as she's in her seat, she takes the Bible out of the cover and starts to read out loud to anyone who will listen. It doesn't matter to her whether she's reading the concordance or from the Old Testament—the story she's telling is one she's learned in Sunday school."

Debbie, on the other hand, had a different experience. She grew up the youngest of four children, and the only daughter. "My parents were never churchgoers," she says, "but I was always taught right from wrong. They did encourage us to attend church, but of the four of us, I think I was the only one who attended on a consistent basis. However, I left my church when I was about thirteen because I thought there were too many man-made rules. But I found a church that I liked after I married, and that is where my two daughters were baptized. I have allowed my daughters to discover their own sense of religion, and they have attended all types of services. They seem just as curious about the different rules as I was. When it comes down to it, though, we all come back to the Bible and our own personal interpretation. We use the church setting as a way to gain fellowship, not necessarily as our sole guide in our relationship with God."

Finding the Sacred in Everyday Things

There are beautiful, everyday moments that are sacred and should be kept close in our hearts. These moments appear without warning, so we must keep our hearts and minds open to catch them as they dash through our busy days. A mother travels quickly through life as she raises daughters into women. Her sacred moment might be listening to her child say her bedtime prayers, as she asks God to care for Mama, Daddy, and little brother—or it might be a glance out the kitchen window, watching one daughter comfort another with a newly skinned knee. Did your little girl ever find a bird who'd fallen out of a nest and bring it home for you to care for? Has she asked you why babies sometimes go to heaven? These are sacred, everyday moments that surely express the meaning of spirituality and the true measure of a daughter's heart.

Meditation and Inspiration

I'm convinced that spending time alone every day is essential to having good mental and spiritual health. Sometimes we need to step back from everyday concerns, empty our minds of the background noise of day-to-day living, and experience some quiet, reflective time. Repetitive, rhythmic activities can be used to free our minds to wander in whatever direction they may. When we let our thoughts flow in a relaxed state, we are sorting out old information and searching for new ideas and solutions on a deeper level. Just as dreaming allows your unconscious to work out problems, a quiet, meditative state can inspire creative thought. It's best to connect with a practice that comes from your heart, not because someone recommended it. When you find one you connect with, make it part of your life. A consistent practice will deepen your experience and lead you to spiritual renewal. Here are a few examples of repetitive actions that may help you reach a relaxed and spiritual state of mind:

- *Walking, jogging, swimming laps, or yoga*
- *Gardening of all kinds*
- *Drawing, painting, and sculpting*
- *Hand quilting or sewing, spinning, weaving, knitting, crocheting, and basketmaking*
- *Repeating a mantra (a phrase, saying, or word) while in a relaxed state is a practice utilized by many religions and spiritual groups worldwide*
- *Deep-breathing exercises while sitting motionless with eyes closed*
- *Silent prayer*

PART FIVE

Home Arts

Chapter 16

Making a House a Home

When we hear the words "Welcome home," each of us may have a different image of the physical characteristics of home, but our feelings about what a home should be will be quite similar. A home should be comfortable, peaceful, have an inviting ambience, and serve as an oasis from life's storms and a place to simply *be*. Home is where you belong, where you have special rights and privileges, and release from the pressures of the outside world. The sense of feeling at home is important to our well-being, and if we don't get enough of this warm feeling, we probably won't feel happy or content. Home also provides you with something no other place can—your history.

There are certain houses you live in all your life—your childhood home, with all its memories; a college dorm, with its roommates and rites of passage; your first apartment rented with money from your first real job; and the place you chose as your own family's first home. I don't think we ever really move away from any of these places. Instead, we carry them around like blocks, building one upon the other, as we go through life. Traditionally, the center of family has been the home, and throughout history women have often served as the home's CEO. They have wielded a commanding presence, kept track of smaller subenterprises, delegated and supervised work, and been responsible for teaching, counseling, and the physical and emotional well-being of the family unit. To carry the analogy further, men have traditionally shouldered responsibility for financing the operation and, in the latter part of the twentieth century, took their place as second-in-command. But recent years have seen great changes in home life. Today, women spend less time at home and are CEOs of *other* organizations.

No matter our job, what dreams we're following, or the glass ceiling we've shattered, we and our daughters need to live in more than just a house or apartment—we need to live in a *home*. Away from home, we have deadlines, situations, and people to deal with, pressures, and stress. We need to come home to an entirely different environment. Our homes should offer inviting possibilities for places to be alone, have intimate chats, read or study, play games, watch movies, or engage in other pastimes that reinforce and refresh our inner lives.

Decorating

Making a house a home is certainly about decorating; however, it's also about creating an environment that meets our individual needs. We all have special qualities that make a home our own, but ultimately, a home life should be rich in companionship and creativity. Instead of worrying about decorating, surround yourself with things that open up all your senses:

- *Fabrics or objects with interesting textures*
- *Calming colors—soft blues, greens, and natural tones*
- *Things that are pleasing to the eye—artwork, personal keepsakes, and collections such as seashells, handcrafted baskets, or pottery*
- *The renewing essence of aroma-therapy candles*
- *The scents of fresh flowers and greenery*
- *Sounds you find soothing—like classical music or a CD of the sounds of nature or the ocean*

Remember, no matter the size of your home, your family, or your pocketbook, you can turn your house into a safe haven—a place that embodies the personal touch that only you, your mother, and your daughter can provide. One place to look for inspiration in creating decorating schemes and providing finishing touches is nature's colors, textures, and scents:

- *Choose a theme, like water, which is reflected in shades of blue, teal, green, white, and silver—or the woods, with every shade of brown and green, earth tones, and richly textured fabrics.*
- *Write down all the colors and textures you can think of and try to match them with decorating ideas such as paint, wallpaper, fabric, lamps and shades, accessories, and knickknacks.*
- *Bring nature into your home to create a sense of awareness of the world outside. Collect seashells or small crystals and display them on a mirror. Study different types of geodes and rough quartz, and learn how they're formed.*

The Kitchen

If you don't have a focal point to your home or a place where people "hang out," the kitchen is a logical choice. If someone is in the kitchen cooking, other members of the household will gravitate there to help, chat, or just see what's for dinner. Having a nearby seating area also encourages people to sit and talk.

I first met Patricia over twenty years ago when we worked together, and although we now live a long distance apart, we're still good friends. Patricia grew up in a warm, loving home and has fond memories of her mother's kitchen: "As I was growing up, I remember drinking hot tea with my mother at lunchtime. On these occasions, when it was just the two of us, there was an opportunity to discuss problems or concerns I was having, or that she had with me. Preparing and sharing a pot of English tea has become a ritual shared by my mother and me, my daughter and me, and my daughter and her grandmother. This simple tradition has led to our sharing intimate thoughts or reminiscing about the past."

Many people entertain and have guests in their kitchens rather than their dining rooms because a kitchen feels relaxed and evokes warm, cozy memories. Maybe it goes back to our childhoods, when Mom was cooking our favorite dinner or teaching us how to make pancakes. For many people, a kitchen means love, home cooking, and Mom. If you haven't created kitchen traditions with your daughter, start with a few of these ideas:

- *Sit down together for breakfast during the week, even if it's for only ten minutes, and start a conversation about anything at all. See where it takes you.*
- *If your teenage daughter does homework in her bedroom, invite her to use the kitchen table by using it yourself. Do paperwork, write letters, make "to do" lists, or engage in any activity that can be easily interrupted.*
- *No matter what you're cooking or putting together for dinner, ask your daughter for help. Working together creates an intimacy that fosters communication.*

Deborah, a mathematician, helped her mother in the kitchen when she was a child. "It was often my job to lay the table, because I didn't mind doing it, and because I was good at it. I made sure the tablecloth was clean and evenly spread out, and I made sure to fold the napkins nicely. I'm sure that originally Mum had taught me how to do it, but I just can't remember that because I've been doing it for so long. I'm now teaching my daughters how to set the table, where each fork goes, how to place the knives, which side the glass and salad plate go, and other things."

Many people don't sit down to dinner anymore, and as a result we're forgetting these lessons in etiquette. I'm not too big on formality, but we should teach these skills to our children and make them a time-honored tradition in our homes.

The Boudoir

People tend to keep things that are close to their hearts in the bedroom—diaries and journals, love letters, precious photographs or mementos and tokens of loyalty and affection—and tuck them away in drawers and trunks. A boudoir should be a place of rest, refuge, and intimacy. It should have a "soft touch." You want a place where you can escape the worries of the day, and that's likely to come most easily in a room that feels *right* to you, however it looks or feels to anyone else.

When I was a young girl, my sister and I shared a bedroom, but when I was fifteen we moved to a bigger house, and I finally got a room of my own. My mother let me decorate it myself, but kept me to a budget. I chose pink paint for the walls (and painted them myself), a tailored bedspread in deep cherry, and five or six small pillows in shades of pink, rose, cherry, and white for the bed. The last of my budget was used for a white wicker clothes hamper and wastebasket. I can remember going through my keepsakes and mementos to find things to put out "for show"—a heart-shaped porcelain container for my seashell collection, a basket for the antique buttons I'd gleaned from my grandmother's sewing box, strands of beads to drape over the lampshade, and, of course, posters of my favorite rock stars. I loved that room. It spoke to me, and of me, because I had created an intimate space that met my needs and *made me feel at home.*

Now help your daughter create a place where she can dream. Let her imagination guide her. Encourage her to include a comfortable, overstuffed chair, a good reading lamp, and a writing table with room for a few of her favorite books, a writing journal, and a pot of tea.

Collections

Deborah loves her coffee table. She purchased an unfinished square table with three shallow drawers, and whitewashed the wood. The top has glass, so you can see what is inside the top drawer. It's the perfect place for a collection. "I have the drawer lined with felt and change the contents with the seasons. Right now, it has a collection of shells we got from the beach last year, some little books, postcards, and other summer mementos. When you walk into the den, this is one of the first things you notice because you glimpse something under the glass. That's what draws you over to see more. It's a conversation piece when we have visitors, and gives me an opportunity to share family stories.

"During Christmas, I line it with red felt and scatter photos of past Christmases and a few antique ornaments. This prompts my daughters to ask to hear stories about certain holidays, like the Christmas we got Freckles, our dog, and I had to stay up all night to keep her quiet, or the Christmas my daughter was one month old. This year I'm going to ask my mom for some old photos of Christmas when I was a child and include those in my drawer, along with the antique ornaments that belonged to my grandmother. I feel they are safer in the drawer than on the tree until my children are a little older. I even have the original box she kept them in, with the price still written on top—ninety-nine cents for twelve."

Nostalgia helps create a homey feel to any room. Framing a collection of old photos or mementos from childhood, a vacation, or past holidays will make you feel good, add intimacy to the room, and brighten your day.

Home Arts Program

Lee has five daughters and homeschools the youngest three (two have already gone off to college). We were both members of an Internet E-mail list when she first wrote a post about the home arts program she'd arranged for a group of mothers and daughters. I was intrigued and asked her to write about what she was doing.

"Our Home Arts group was mothers and daughters working together. My motive behind the group was practical—to teach the girls homemaking skills that so few learn today. This area of study has been a particular interest of mine all my life. When I was sixteen, I was digging up roots to make sassafras tea, and experimenting with wild foods. When I went off to college, I took my mother's old Betty Crocker cookbook and Singer sewing machine. Over the next few years, in between microbiology classes, I taught myself to sew. I lived in a trailer and had a kitchen, so I practiced my cooking on anybody who came over. The second summer, I bought a canner so I could preserve the blackberries growing around the trailer. Looking back, the really funny part of all this is that I never planned to get married, have children, or do all those traditional things. Years later, I decided my children would all learn these skills while I was here to teach them.

"Part of my homeschooling requirements for my daughters are basic kitchen skills: making a white sauce, biscuits, cakes, pies, and yeast breads; planning and cooking meals; and sewing at least one garment without my help. Another skill I teach them is how to be thrifty, using the old adage 'Use it up, wear it out, make it do, or do without,' that my mother often quoted. I wanted to make sure that even if times were hard, my girls could cope. This type of training takes time, but it pays off.

"It's so hard to convince people to take the time to learn home arts, and I wish I could convince more people to pass on their skills. My own mother didn't, because though she was a talented and imaginative person who loved her job of homemaker, she didn't consider those things to be worth much compared to formal education. Although she died when I was fifteen, my mother passed on to me a sense of joy about keeping a home that stayed with me, even when I was a professional career woman."

Lee's home arts plan is quite extensive because it was part of a homeschooling program that met almost every week. You could tailor a smaller program to meet your needs and the needs of your daughter, or you could compare notes with other moms and daughters who are interested in joining forces. Here's Lee's home arts program, which you can use as a blueprint for your own:

- Pressure canning: *Learning the basic techniques with a dial-type pressure canner using pinto beans. Waiting time will be spent peeling apples, quilting, cross-stitching, knitting, and making apple dumplings.*
- Mending: *Learning basic mending skills and techniques. If time permits, peel more apples and pears, or work on needlework.*
- Water bath canning: *Basic techniques of making applesauce by using the water bath method. Work on needlework if time allows.*
- Beginning Patchwork: *The girls will begin piecing at least one quilt patch from the patch patterns provided (Shoofly, Snowball, Basic Nine-Patch, and Friendship Star). The blocks are all nine inches with quarter-inch seams. Continue working on blocks during spare time at future meetings.*
- Making noodles: *Make egg noodles in different widths by learning the steps involved in making the dough and running it through the pasta machine.*
- Breadmaking: *The girls will learn to make several different kinds of bread by hand methods.*
- Quilting: *With interest running high, the girls will work on their accumulation of blocks. At this meeting, each girl can decide what her goal will be—pot holders; twin, full, or queen-size quilt; a wall hanging, or . . .? Should all the blocks be the same, or how about a sampling of patterns? Mothers can help, start their own quilts, or work on another sewing project.*
- Making pies: *Get ready for the holiday season! Make*

up a big batch of dough, and roll out pies, mini-pies, or half-moon pies, depending on your preferences.

- Baking cookies: *Bring a variety of cookie cutters, and learn to make dough for several different varieties.*
- Gift making for the holidays: *Work on cinnamon-applesauce ornaments and apple or orange pomanders, making dough for the cinnamon ornaments ahead of time. Bring cloves, cinnamon, apples, and an orange or two. The ornaments are a very nice "country touch" that even Martha Stewart would approve of. They are rolled out like cookies, baked, and can be used as fragrant decorations or package tie-ons.*
- Holiday cookie exchange: *Bring six dozen cookies of the fancier varieties, and put out a dozen for sampling. Exchange the other five dozen, so the girls go home with a nice selection of cookies for the holidays.* (Note: the girls should be the primary planners and cooks!) Meanwhile, put the finishing touches on any holiday projects, and discuss what to do the second half of the year.

Here are some additional ideas:

- *Make up bags of soup or seasoned rice mix, and package them in cloth bags the girls sew and tie with ribbons.*
- *Soap making*
- *Knitting*
- *Book repair*
- *Creative memories (scrapbook pages)*
- *Planning a garden*
- *Making aprons*
- *Dollmaking*

Although you might think a home arts plan sounds old-fashioned, I'd ask you to consider the rewards of such a program:

- *You will have good, quality time with your daughter.*
- *Teaching can be divided among several women with varied skills.*
- *Your daughter will develop long-lasting friendships with the other girls, and you with the other moms.*
- *She can put these skills to use now—and later, when she has a home of her own.*

Daughters learn so much at their mothers' knees, and building a close relationship is essential if we are to pass on the skills and instincts that are important in making a house a home. Remember, many aspects of the homes our daughters will create for their own families will be based on the childhood homes they remember.

Chapter 17

Mother's Recipes

I have a confession to make. I love to cook. In today's fast-paced world, where time is money, it's easy to latch on to the idea that cooking is old-fashioned. However, I'd like to change that impression. Last fall I noticed a sign on a familiar fast-food outlet that read "You'd be crazy to cook!" I wasn't surprised, but I was annoyed. I knew the purpose of the ad wasn't to put good, healthful food on any family's table, or to provide an opportunity for families to come together at least once a day for all the right reasons. The purpose of that ad was to increase sales of fast food— and to deemphasize home cooking.

Good meals at home can satisfy more than just physical hunger—they can satisfy the emotions, too. When we think back on childhood memories, Mom's cooking is usually one of the first things that come to mind. When I miss my mother, one of the places I miss her most is in the kitchen. The memories of her cooking for our family make me feel warm inside and give me the feeling of being cared for and loved. I think today's children deserve those kinds of memories as they're growing up, too. We all know cooking isn't just about food—it's about relationships, nurturing, doing something for others (if you're the cook), and feeling taken care of and appreciated (if you're being cooked for).

The smell and taste of familiar food evoke strong memories of mothers and grandmothers who spent hours making everything from scratch, of family meals that became traditions, or of special occasions at which favorite dishes were the highlight of the meal. Today, we don't have to spend hours preparing a good meal unless we truly want to. There are plenty of cooking methods and products that can decrease the time needed to put a good, nutritious meal on the table.

The Center of a Home

The kitchen has been the center of the home for generations. It's not just a place to cook, it's a place to learn about life, do homework, catch up on events of the day, give and get both praise and scoldings, and solve problems. You can have a tea party with your little girl and entice a teenager out of her bedroom with the smell of chocolate chip cookies warm from the oven. If your daughter's decided to become a vegetarian or wants to visit Paris next summer, get cozy in the kitchen with a cookbook and try out new recipes together. The sharing of skills, talents, laughter, joy, anguish, and tears—that's what a kitchen is all about. When we cook with our mothers' recipes, we are re-creating the time, attention, and love she gave us when we were children. We are also remembering with our hands what our hearts already know.

Mary Beth is one of three sisters. They're all close but live long distances from one another. Mary Beth feels a major focus of their continuing relationship revolves around the kitchen—not just every day but for celebrations, too: "Every holiday, the phone rings off the hook to ask advice on just how to make Mom's Polish holiday bread. 'Mine's not rising well. What should I do?' 'They only had cake yeast at the store. How much should I use?' 'I can't find the recipe. Can you send me a copy?' It really keeps us connected at holidays though the miles may separate us."

Natural or By-the-Book Cooks

The centers of our lives should be our home and family. The foods that "taste like home" also make us feel happy and secure and give us a sense of identity. Family recipes have a connection to the past because they've been handed down from mother to daughter. Recipes might be kept in organized notebooks, found in battered copies of a favorite cookbook that has a broken binding and notes written in the margins, on index cards, or in handwritten recipes.

I have fond memories of my mother's cooking, even though special meals were saved for weekends because she had a career. She's what I call a "natural cook" in that she has a comprehensive grasp of basic cooking skills and ingredients, what goes with what, and how to enhance the taste of foods. She also has the knack for throwing together a tasteful, balanced meal with just about anything, or practically nothing. My sister and I were always welcome in the kitchen. Mom had no qualms about handing over a dish to a curious ten-year-old or encouraging us to experiment with the intriguing jars lining the spice rack. Of course, that led to some pretty interesting meals, but that's what teaching and learning are all about.

Like many natural cooks, Pat's mother didn't use recipes, and that's what turned Pat into an advocate of keeping track of those favorite family recipes. "Food does bring back a lot of childhood memories for each of us, different foods in different generations. My mother rarely used recipes, except for baking. She always made my grandmother's mustard salad dressing when we had relatives over for dinner, and I had to watch her make it and attempt to measure the ingredients she was putting in so I could make up a recipe for myself."

Marni's grandmother didn't use recipes either. She was also an incredible baker who started the tradition in Marni's family: "My mother wanted to learn how to bake like her mother did, but Grandma never measured anything and Mom couldn't do it by look and feel. So she tried holding measuring cups and spoons under the ingredients as her mother was adding them to the dough, but then Grandma could no longer get a good sense of how the dough was coming together, so Mom never did become a baker. When I was a young adult, I happened on a brochure put

Rugelach

1 pound unsalted butter
½ pound cream cheese
3½ cups flour
3 tablespoons sour cream
¼ cup sugar
½ teaspoon salt
16 ounces orange marmalade or jam
½ cup chopped walnuts

Cream the butter and cream cheese together. Add the flour, sour cream, sugar, and salt. Knead into a dough and refrigerate several hours until firm. Roll into 9-inch circles, using about ⅙ of the dough for each circle. Combine the marmalade or jam and chopped walnuts (or cinnamon-sugar and walnuts) and spread on circles of dough. Cut each circle into 8 wedge-shaped sections. Roll each wedge, starting from the large end and ending with the point. Curve to form a crescent shape, placing the open end down on a buttered baking sheet. Bake at 375° for 15 minutes or until browned. Makes 4 dozen.

Here are some cooking tips from Marni: "I often make these smaller and less crescent-shaped—just rolled and cut into 1- to 2-inch lengths. You should refrigerate the dough when it's not being worked as it gets really soft very quickly."

out by a grocery store containing Jewish recipes. I tried the rugelach [a filled pastry] recipe and was amazed to discover that it was pretty darn close to my grandma's. Rugelach has become my regular holiday 'cookie.' My daughter is now the family baker. When she was twelve, she asked for the book *Baking with Julia* for a Hanukkah present and has made several of the recipes, including an amazing puff pastry."

Kitchen Memories

Mistie describes herself as "a college student, full-time mom, wife, cook, cleaner, taxi driver, nurse, financial adviser, accountant, and general all-purpose buffer between family and the outside world." When I asked her to think back on fond childhood memories in the kitchen, she said, "I remember when my dad would be away from home, Mom would always make breakfast for supper. We loved it, and it was so much easier for my mom, as she had three kids to feed and keep entertained." Mistie's husband is in the military, so she's keeping the tradition of "breakfast for supper" with her daughter, Alexis: "My daughter and I love breakfast, so we use every excuse to eat it. My favorite is the omelet, followed closely by scrambled eggs with cheese and onions, home-cooked potatoes (the ones cut like silver dollars), bacon, and sometimes pancakes or French toast. Favorites from childhood were potatoes smothered in ketchup and 'garbage.' "

Cultural and Ethnic Cooking

Ethnic groups from around the globe continue to spread their recipes and kitchen traditions as increasing tourism brings foreign cuisines home. It used to be that Mexican, French, Italian, Chinese, and Japanese foods were the most prevalent here in the United States; but now you can find a restaurant or cookbook that reflects the culture of almost any ethnicity. Foreign and home-grown recipes are even easier to access now that we have the Internet.

Michelle has one daughter, Katie. "My family is such a mix—my grandfather is Jewish and my grandmother Methodist, so it wasn't unusual for us to have a Sunday dinner of fried chicken and lox. I hope if Katie learns

Breakfast "Garbage"

½ raw onion, finely chopped
1 cup cooked hash browns
Oil or butter
4 eggs
½ cup cheddar cheese
3 slices bacon, fried and
    crumbled
Salt and pepper to taste
5 or 6 flour tortillas

Brown the onions and hash browns in a few tablespoons of oil or butter in a skillet. Mix eggs together, pour into skillet, and stir until done, adding cheese, bacon, and salt and pepper when done. Put the mixture on flour tortillas, fold one end, roll, and eat.
Serves 5 or 6.
A cooking note from Mistie: "You can add other ingredients, such as chopped green or red peppers, sliced mushrooms, etc. Sometimes we also enjoyed this dish with homemade black peppery gravy smothered over the top."

nothing else, it's that our society is such a mix of cultures, and we have to work with and among them all.

"We eat a lot of good food straight from our garden, including chicken that my grandmother raises. I don't know that anyone really taught me how to cook; I think it came naturally from watching everyone over the years. My family tended to congregate in the kitchen. I try to keep Katie with me while I'm cooking, and she has developed a taste for a wide variety of foods from different cultures."

Comfort Foods

Comfort foods are sometimes given a bad name because they're usually high in carbohydrates. Nevertheless, these foods still seem to fill our need to be nourished, nurtured, and satisfied. Magically, they impart a feeling of physical and emotional well being.

Pat grew up with milk gravy for Sunday breakfast after her family came home from church. "It was a thick gravy made from bacon grease and flour mixed in a roux. Then milk was added slowly and the gravy was stirred constantly until it thickened to the right consistency. The gravy was poured over white bread and topped with crumbled bacon and chopped raw onion. The roots for this dish might lie somewhere back in my grandfather's Pennsylvania Dutch ancestry or maybe during the Great Depression. When my mom was young, it was made with salt pork because they couldn't afford bacon. Needless to say, we don't make this much anymore for health reasons, but even my husband developed a taste for it over the years."

Comfort foods are also easy to make, and that certainly isn't bad for anyone. Think about oatmeal with raisins and walnuts—as soon as you hold a bowl in your hands, it warms your senses and gives you fuel to get through the day. Same with a hearty stew or Tuscan bean soup served with warm biscuits or toasted French bread topped with cheddar cheese.

Chicken and dumplings are also comfort food, and Michelle's mother cooked a variation called "slippery-down potpie" that her two daughters love. "We would always have heavily cured country ham, turkey, and all the trimmings, rolls, lots of pies and Jell-O salads, and slippery-down potpie. This potpie was more like soup or stew and was made from chicken, potatoes, onions, broth, and seasonings. A dough similar to pie crust was cut into one inch squares, added to the broth, and cooked till done—almost like dumplings. Slippery-down potpie is eaten ladled on the plate and served with thick slices of bread and butter. My father often requested slippery-down during the winter. It was probably a comfort food for him since he spent a lot of time on the farm with his grandparents. My mother, having learned how to make it from her mother-in-law, would make it for him all the time." Michelle's mother also taught her how to cook this favorite recipe that's been a tradition in their family for two generations.

Learning to Cook

Tammy, thirty, loves to have her two little girls in the kitchen, and together they've established their own holiday cooking traditions: "On Valentine's Day we always have a romantic dinner for the whole family, and I make bread and color it with red food coloring. The girls help decide the menu and also prepare the meal. St. Patrick's Day is always green milk, green mashed potatoes, and chicken. We also have green ice cream. On Easter, we make an Easter bunny cake (which I did with my mother), candy, and have a big neighborhood egg hunt. This is an event we started when we moved into our new home and thought it would be a nice way to meet our neighbors."

Tammy, mother of six, gourmet cook, and gardener, developed her interest in cooking while spending her youth with her stand-in mom, Aunt Orie, who was an important part of her childhood. "I still vividly remember standing on the vinyl kitchen chair, pushed up to the counter and cutting biscuit dough with a small juice glass. She gave me my own special pan that was small, like my special cutter, so I could make miniature biscuits to my heart's content. As an adult, I have often wondered just how much Aunt Orie had to adjust her recipes to compensate for all the dough that went into my mouth."

I'm sure Tammy's Aunt Orie didn't mind. After all, tasting is part of learning to cook. Since most little girls like sweets, an easy way to bring your daughter into the kitchen is to start with cake. Here are a few tips for an easy "first time" in the kitchen:

- *Use a packaged cake mix in her favorite flavor.*
- *Read the directions out loud.*
- *Show her how to measure ingredients.*
- *Depending on her age, you might want to operate the mixer, but be sure and let her lick the beaters and mixing spoon.*
- *Let her help oil and flour the pans, and pour the batter.*
- *When it's time to check if the cake is done, put the pan on the counter and let her insert a toothpick in the cake to see if it comes out "clean."*

I believe most little girls learn a lot of things from their mothers because moms are their role models, and this goes for when they're young and when they're older, too. So, remember how your daughter admires you, and try to curb any impatience you might have, especially when it comes to batter getting everywhere but in the bowl or cake pan. Here are a few more ideas for learning to cook with your mother or daughter:

- *Check with your local community college, adult continuing education, state university extension office, or private cooking schools for classes at all levels of instruction and in different cuisines that you and your mom can take together.*
- *Read one of the many cookbooks on the market that*

target beginning cooks, teenagers and adults, including Betty Crocker's Cooking Basics.

- *Any of the Williams-Sonoma series on cooking will take you a step farther, with volumes on everything from breads to Mediterranean cooking to vegetables. You and your daughter can explore these with each other.*
- Family Fun's Cookbook—250 Irresistible Recipes for You and Your Kids *will help you make learning to cook a family affair.*

Chapter 18

Canning and Food Preservation

$\mathcal{T}$hroughout history, people have found ways to preserve food so they could enjoy the bounty of the harvest and abundant game during times when supplies were scarce. In the early 1800s, French scientist and chef Nicolas Appert first preserved food on a commercial level to help the French army alleviate the problem of losing troops due to malnutrition. The first principles for food processing and preserving used heat and closed containers. Based on these methods, Louis Pasteur developed the process of pasteurization. Glass mason jars and threaded tops were first invented in 1858, and the pressure canner followed in 1874.

The art of canning hasn't changed much since those times, but it has become somewhat of a lost art during the last few decades. As supermarkets systematically replaced root cellars and gardens, people began purchasing more and more of their food, rather than growing or preparing it themselves.

Many people get interested in food preservation when they decide to start their own gardens and find themselves with more produce than their families can eat—or give away. Others are concerned about the health issues of eating processed foods, or simply enjoy being in the kitchen and serving truly homemade meals. No matter what your reason, home canning isn't as difficult as you might think, and it's the perfect way to share your favorite tastes with your mother and daughter, family and friends. If you have the old-fashioned idea that canning and preserving turn out tasteless or boring food, you're way off base. There are thousands of recipes that you, your mom, and your daughter can choose from—anything from jams and jellies to zesty condiments like salsa or chutney, or flavorful vegetables to brandied fruits.

Preserving Love

Lyn, a family nurse practitioner, learned how to can foods from her mother. "Canning will probably become 'nouvel' or a 'retro' thing to do, but around here, it is just something we do every year. Once the gardens start producing, canning supplies spill into the living room because there's always something to 'put up.' One of our favorite things to do is tomatoes, and my mom and I generally do them together. Of course, since Mom has a Virgo rising, there are certain procedures to be followed. First, all tomatoes have to be washed, sorted, checked for bruising, and de-stemmed. Next, blanch the tomatoes in boiling water for exactly three minutes, then remove to a sink of ice water. Next comes peeling, which is the most tedious part. However, to do it properly, one must core and *then* peel, since coring is crucial to remove any tough pieces. Then, they go into the jars, and an assembly line is established to put the hot water over them (my job), wipe the jars and check head space (Mom's job), and put on the lids and rings (a friend's job).

"The real reason we can so many tomatoes is not because we eat a ton but because we want to be together. This is the time we can talk about how things used to be done and how important it is to put your energy into food preparation. When we feed our family, we would rather use things we have blessed with our sweat, energy, and love than throw something on the table from a bag with no idea if it has been cooked properly or is good for us. Even cookies are better when made from scratch. I believe that when we can food, we aren't just preserving the vegetables or fruit, we are also preserving love and caring for our families. I have a four-year-old nephew who will only eat the pickled beets that I make. He says it makes him feel special that I make them for him, and it makes me feel special that he only likes the ones I make.

"Over the years, we have giggled at my mom's insistence that the tomatoes be just so. Although we may tease my mom about how particular she is about doing things properly, she's the one I always call with questions because she has the answers. She knows the 'infrastructure' of canning, and I want to preserve that, too."

A Family Affair

Marlene, a former teacher and tax accountant, and now a textile artist, has fond childhood memories of "putting up food." "My mother did a mountain of canning every summer. She would load us four kids in the car and head toward my aunt's home in southern New Jersey. Then we'd go to the 'pick your own' farms. The youngest usually played and ate raspberries while the older kids did a fair share of the picking. Many an afternoon with the cousins on the back porch, we'd be shelling peas or snapping beans. My mother always did her canning in batches, and from my young perspective, it seemed like a gargantuan task."

Peggy and her husband believe in being self-reliant, which includes raising and preserving their own food: "We always had a big garden, and I would can hundreds of quarts of fruits and vegetable, soups and meats. We raised our own animals, too, but we had to buy hay and grain for feed, so we also worked outside the home. Somehow, we also managed to raise three daughters and two sons—all good kids who worked alongside us. I remember one Thanksgiving in particular, when all the delicious food we served was produced at home, and we were all so proud of that."

The Freshest Produce

The first rule in putting up fruits or vegetables, whether canning, drying, preserving, pickling, or freezing, is to use the freshest produce that is either perfectly ripe or slightly underripe. Maureen, a kindergarten teacher, gardened with her mother when she was a girl, and now her daughter, Celeste, shares her passion for red, ripe tomatoes, the greenest peppers and zucchini, deep purple eggplants, and dozens of other vegetables fresh-picked from their garden. "What I love most about having my own garden is that I'm able to put up small batches of vegetables when they're at their height of taste and flavor. Celeste is only nine, but she's a great help picking the best veggies, chopping and dicing, and putting on the labels once I take the jars out of the canner. She loves to see the rows of jars on the pantry shelf, and helps choose what to eat next."

If you don't have a garden, you can still obtain fresh fruits and vegetables during the growing season at farmers' markets, at some health food stores, or at small independent grocers or co-ops that buy directly from farms.

New Twists on an Old Idea

Doris, a decorator who enjoys cooking, has one daughter, Gracie, who is fourteen. "Gracie sees no use in canning practical things like tomatoes. She kept trying to get me to try more unusual recipes like relishes, marmalades, or chutneys made with ginger, mangoes, and exotic spices. I took her advice and bought all the ingredients for one of the chutneys and coaxed her into helping me. Now we process foods together, and enjoy seeing all our colorful jars line the shelf. An added benefit is that I can put together a good, nutritious meal pretty quickly."

If canning or drying food seems old-fashioned to you, maybe it's because you're thinking green beans, tomatoes, or dried bananas. Creative cooks and new recipes are taking the basics and expanding them into a variety of flavors, textures, and colors. Here are a few ways to start spicing things up:

- *Follow your cravings—do you pine for sweet, plump fruit when there's snow on the ground? How about fall vegetables in early spring?*

- *Explore new tastes—gooseberries, currants, prickly pears, elderberries, dried salmon, or lamb jerky.*
- *Pair up ingredients—instead of apple butter, try apple-pear butter, instead of just green beans, add slices of lemon peel.*

Safety

Robin, a stay-at-home mom, bought her produce from a farmers' market for years before deciding to try canning. She read a book on basic canning techniques and decided to take a course offered by her state university extension office. "I didn't realize that there were so many safety issues, and I wanted to make sure I knew what I was doing. In no time at all, I got the hang of it, and have enjoyed canning fruit and vegetables ever since."

Microorganisms are present in all fresh foods, and it is very important to follow canning directions carefully so foods are processed long enough at the right temperature to destroy these microorganisms. Spoiled canned food can cause serious health problems, so if you have any question about food you've canned, follow the old axiom: "If in doubt, throw it out." Here are a few telltale signs that something is wrong:

- *A lid that has not sealed correctly or that is bulging*
- *A noticeable discoloration in the food, especially a darker color*
- *Mold in the food, inside the lid, or on the outside of the jar*
- *Small bubbles in the liquid*
- *Changes in the texture of the food*

Preserving

Jams, jellies, preserves, fruit butters, and marmalades that you preserve yourself taste infinitely better than commercial products and are wonderful gifts for family and friends. Although there are more tricks to making jellies and jams, fruit butters are a sure bet for the beginner. You don't have to worry about jelling at all, because fruit butters are a thick puree that can be made in a slow cooker like a Crock-Pot.

Although Anne's mother made preserves when she was a child, Anne has limited time and has found fruit butters a nice substitute for that homemade taste: "Fruit butters have an intense flavor that we like in the morning on toast or muffins. When it's time for another batch, both my daughters help out, and we end up spending a nice afternoon together. My daughter Tiffany is in Girl Scouts and has asked me to teach her troop this summer. I'm afraid I may find myself with quite a production on my hands, but I've decided to go ahead with the project. If I can get a few moms to help out, we'll be able to pass on these 'old' skills to a new generation."

Crock-Pot Apple Butter

3 quarts tart apples
4 cups sugar
⅓ cup apple cider
½ teaspoon cinnamon
½ teaspoon cloves

Peel, core, and cut the apples into small pieces. Put the fruit, sugar, and cider into a Crock-Pot or other slow cooker and cook on high for 2 hours. Turn to low and cook for 6 to 8 hours. Add the spices during the last hour of cooking. Scoop into a blender a few cups at a time and blend 2 to 3 minutes. Return the mixture to the Crock-Pot and cook on high until the fruit butter reaches the desired thickness. Scoop into jars and store, covered, in the refrigerator.

Dehydration

Drying is an easy, space-saving way to make delicious snacks, seasonings, and convenience foods. The variety of items you can create by dehydration is terrific—fruit leathers, veggie chips, herbs, and jerky sticks are just a start. When you dry foods, you simply remove the water content to create a highly concentrated product with more flavor and nutrients, pound for pound, than fresh food.

Better yet, when dried properly, these foods can't go bad—because bacteria, yeast, and mold can't live without moisture. You can dry food outdoors in the sunlight in protected drying trays, in your oven, in a microwave, or in an inexpensive dehydrator (available at general merchandise stores like Wal-Mart or Sears).

Sally uses her dehydrator for drying her daughters' favorite dried fruit leather and veggie chips: "My girls are only six and seven, but they still help by arranging slices on the trays and making sure there's plenty of space between each one so the air can circulate. They love telling their friends they helped make the snacks they take to school in their lunch boxes. My mother wasn't real handy in the kitchen, and didn't teach me to cook at all. I don't have the kind of memories I'm making with my girls, but I'm glad we're making them together. I've dried vegetables, fruit, and meat in my dehydrator, but my all-time favorite is tomatoes. We love them, and I just can't see paying the price for store-bought sun-dried tomatoes."

Sun-Dried Tomatoes

Slice tomatoes in thirds and place cut side up on trays in a dehydrator set at 120° for about 24 hours. They're done when leathery but pliable. Store in glass jars with tight lids and crumble over pasta or use in sauces or dressings. To rehydrate, let stand in boiling water for a few minutes until they reach a chewy consistency.

Equipment and Resources

There are basically three types of canners: water bath, pressure, and steam. The water bath method is used for foods that are high in acid; pressure canning is used for low-acid foods; and steam can be used instead of the water bath method for acidic foods such as tomatoes, fruits, and pickles. Most experts consider water bath canning safer than steam.

Here's a list of equipment you'll need to get started:

- *Jars and lids*
- *Canner*
- *Strainer*
- *Wide-mouth funnel*
- *Jar lifter*
- *Labels*
- *Ladles*
- *Large bowls*
- *Pots and pans*
- *Long-handled spoons*
- *Slotted spoons*
- *Measuring cups and spoons*
- *Sharp knives*
- *Thermometer*
- *Timer*
- *Vegetable brush*
- *Food processor (optional)*

Here are some resources that will get you, your mother, and your daughter started with the many aspects of preserving food, including techniques, equipment, supplies, and recipes:

- *These two books are perfect for beginners*—Preserving Summer's Bounty: A Quick and Easy Guide to Freezing, Canning, and Preserving, and Drying What You Grow, *by Susan McClure, and* Better Homes and Gardens Presents: America's All-Time Favorite Canning & Preserving Recipes.
- Home Preserver's Magazine *is available by calling 517-592-3905 or subscribing on-line at www.//members.aol.com/preservers/index.html.*

- *The company that manufactures Ball and Kerr home canning products has home economists on staff to answer canning and product-related questions at 800-240-3340 on weekdays during business hours. It also has a free catalog that can be ordered at the same number.*
- *The makers of Sure-Jell and Certo fruit pectin have a help line available weekdays at 800-437-3284.*

Chapter 19

A Garden of Eden

Every garden begins with inspiration and usually has a story to tell. Whether that story is about the designer, the person who did the work, or the plants themselves, a garden can put us in touch with all the senses. Have you ever stepped into a garden and felt stress fall away as if by magic? Did you long to while away the hours absorbing the heady scents, marveling at the riot of color, and touching petals as smooth as silk or as rich as velvet? Whether you're in a flower or vegetable garden in your backyard, on the terrace, or in a public place, gardens have a healing effect and re-connect us with the natural world.

Artists from around the world find inspiration and enthusiasm for color and form in both formal and more natural gardens. Of course, the most famous artist's garden is that of Claude Monet. Monet was a courageous gardener whose desire to learn about color and light turned his countryside garden into a living art form. Renoir also found inspiration for his work in gardens at his farmstead in France. Unlike Monet, who created his personal vision of a garden landscape, Renoir preserved the land and its traditional grassy terraces, vegetable plots, orange trees, and olive groves as a small, verdant remnant of the past. Gardens are infinitely personal, and can be created by you and your mother or daughter to suit whatever form pleases you.

Rose Gardens

My mother was one of those gardeners with a "green thumb." Whatever she planted grew and thrived. Her rose-bushes were always in bloom and were a riot of color in several different shades of red, yellow, pink, white, and a bluish violet I especially liked. My father was in the air force, so we moved every couple of years. But no matter where we lived, one of the first things my mother did was get her hands in the soil, dig, and plant. When we lived in Arizona, we enjoyed roses for six months of the year. My mom's favorite crystal vase graced the dining room table with a dozen blooms, and tiny bud vases with one or two stems were placed in every room. I loved roses so much I never wanted them to fade. But when they did, I collected the petals that fell off the stems and filled a tiny porcelain bowl I kept on my nightstand.

Flower Gardens

Elizabeth, the youngest of four children, now has a baby daughter of her own. Even though she's excited about the joy of sharing traditions with her daughter as she grows up, Elizabeth is saddened by the loss of her mother—to dementia. "I especially treasure links that I do have to the mother I lost somewhere along the way. I like to plant or buy daisies each year because I remember her cutting them fresh from her garden each spring and putting them in a translucent green vase. My favorite pictures of her are where she is beautiful and unstudied, gardening with her daisies in our old backyard. After we moved, she planted all kinds of flowers in the new backyard, even more daisies, but they didn't do as well because there was too much shade. My parents spent many days in their dream house and much time landscaping the yard, planting perennial beds, herb beds, and vegetable gardens. When I was a teenager, and after we had moved several times, my mom and I would go to the nursery together and pick out flowers to set out in the backyard. She let me buy whatever I wanted—begonias, pansies, marigolds, and others I can't recall. We had several gardenia pots on our deck because my mother loved the sweet smell.

"During those teenage years, when we couldn't agree on much, flowers were a sort of common ground for us. I guess she had more time for me then, but I did not usually have time for her. Looking back, there were many times when she tried to give to me but I wasn't ready. These days, I try to give back to her, but because of her dementia I have to seize the moment all the time. Still, I'm thankful that I have concrete memories of things like gardening that remind me of the times we did have. In fact, I have daisies on my table right now because they bring back fond memories of my mother."

Take your daughter on a field trip to a garden nursery. If you're not familiar with gardening, this is a great resource. Choose a nursery with a trained staff, and you can get all the advice you need to grow any variety of plant and any type garden. If you don't have a yard, consider growing flowers on a terrace, a sunny windowsill, or using indoor fluorescent "grow lights."

Tammy spent a lot of her childhood with Aunt Orie and believes her aunt's most influential legacy came from her backyard: "It was a perfect rectangle, with one huge maple to the side. The neighbors' pecan tree hung over the fence. I truly believe this is where my love of gardening began. Aunt Orie showed me how to take an ordinary pink hollyhock and turn it upside down. Suddenly, it was a lady that danced in a saucer of water. Now that I do genealogy as a hobby, I often wonder which mother or aunt passed that on to her daughter, and whether there was a time during the Civil War or the Great Depression when a crying child was comforted by a doll created from a flower by a clever ancestor.

"Aunt Orie's yard would probably be termed today as a cottage-style garden, with a mix of perennials and annuals lining the fence. We used to talk about their fragrance, the different colors, and my favorite—the cockscomb—because it looked like velvet. Aunt Orie was never too busy, nor thought it too silly, for me to talk about how different the rocks felt, which thorns pricked the most, or my favorite color, which was either red or purple, depending on the hour. Her sisters used to admonish her for letting me pick so many flowers, but she told me, 'If God hadn't meant for little girls to pick flowers, he would have never let them bloom.' "

If you've thought about planting a garden and preserving the memories of someone close to your heart, but were overwhelmed by the magnitude of the project, think again. Perhaps the most effective way to start a garden and hold on to memories is to look out your window one day, notice how sunny and warm it is, and think it might be fun to plant a few things and see what happens. From these humble beginnings, gardeners can be born and traditions can grow.

If you don't have a yard, you can still have fresh flowers in your house or office. Buy bouquets from the florist, grocery store, farmers' market, or a street vendor and arrange them yourself. You can even learn the tricks of the trade by reading a book on flower arranging.

Terrariums or Wardian Cases

I discovered terrariums when I was a teenager and fell in love with these miniature gardens under glass. This form of gardening dates back to 1829, when Dr. Nathaniel Ward, a London physician who studied plants as hobby, found that air pollution from nearby factories was killing his ferns. He put some dirt in a jar, planted a few ferns, added water, and discovered that the ferns thrived. That was the beginning of the Victorian fad of displaying elaborate Wardian cases (now generally called terrariums) in formal parlors of the period. Terrariums are the ultimate botanical fascination, they are easy to care for, and they offer a unique way to share the tradition of gardening with your daughter, no matter her age.

Betsy, a high school English teacher, has indoor plants in every room of her house. Yet taking center stage are two terrariums she and her six-year-old daughter worked on together. "My mother always gardened, but since we lived in an apartment, she stuck to indoor plants. I had a small terrarium in my bedroom and remember caring for it myself. I guess that's when I got hooked on bringing nature indoors. Last year, I found Ellen pouring a glass of water into my favorite terrarium. I had a heck of a time draining the water *out* and figured it was time to teach her about plants. Together, we made a terrarium for her room, and she couldn't get over my playing in the dirt with her. We did have fun."

Building a Terrarium

A glass container with a cork or lid
Long-handled tools (available at most nurseries)
Charcoal
Potting soil
Small plants (ferns, moss, lipstick, goldfish, or ivy)

Put ½ inch of charcoal in the bottom of your terrarium to help with drainage. Add a few inches of potting soil and then add plants, putting taller plants in the center and shorter ones to the sides. Add enough water to just dampen the soil. Add rocks or figurines, available in garden nurseries or tropical fish stores, for decoration.

Herbs

From the earliest times, herb gardens have been associated with monasteries, temples, and other religious houses, because herbs were the first known medicinals and religious men and women were the first healers. Members of monastic orders were also the first to write about plants and plant lore, the properties of herbs, and their successes and failures in using herbs for healing. Although some herbs do have healing properties, there is also a lot of folklore that doesn't hold up, so if you have an interest in using herbs medicinally, I strongly suggest researching material that is available in bookstores and on-line.

According to some historians, the first herb garden in America was planted in the 1700s by a Quaker, and herbs were brought into broad use by another religious sect, the Shakers. Although you might know more about their furniture than any of their other products, the Shakers were also known for their highly successful gardening techniques. It was the Shakers who invented the idea of packaging seeds in small packets in order to ensure their freshness and of selling the packets commercially. Herbs can be grown for a variety of uses—cooking, remedies, scents, natural dyeing, or to attract bees and butterflies. In fact, the most potent quality of any good herb garden is its scent. Some herbs smell sweet, pungent, bitter, or aromatic. Highly scented herbs are easily dried and used for potpourris that can be added

Drying Herbs

Tie long-stemmed herbs into loose bunches of five or six stems. If they are bushy, only use two or three stems. For soft-stemmed herbs, or if you're using only the flower heads, spread them on cheesecloth or a screen. For proper drying, air must circulate around the plants, but for really fast drying a microwave will do the job—a minute for small-leaved herbs and up to three minutes for larger varieties. Leaves are ready when they break easily, flowers when they rustle like tissue paper. Store in airtight jars or pots, label and date.

to sachets or used to stuff pillows. Fresh or dried, herbal scents linger, invigorate, and refresh.

Herbs are a unique way to introduce your daughter to the tradition of gardening. They are easy to grow in the backyard or in containers large enough for the balcony or small enough to fit on a sunny windowsill. If you use clay pots, you can make this project even more fun by adding an artistic dimension, like painting fanciful designs on the pots. If you're using herbs for cooking, the difference in taste between fresh and store-bought herbs will amaze you. Here are a few herbs that are easy to grow, harvest, dry, and store:

- *Mint, lemon grass, or chamomile for tea*
- *Feverfew, comfrey, sorrel, Echinacea, and cowslip for medicinal use*
- *The edible flowers of nasturtiums, sweet violets, and calendula*
- *Oregano, basil, thyme, chives, parsley, marjoram, and a variety of sages for cooking*

Vegetable and Fruit Gardens

Karen's mother taught her about gardening, just as her mother

Lavender-Filled Pillow

Fill a pretty pillowcase or cushion cover with dried hops and lavender flowers. Zip up the pillow and place it under your head for a restful afternoon nap or night's sleep. The scent of hops is thought to induce sleep, and that of lavender to relax both body and mind. Every month or two, refresh the mixture by sprinkling with a few drops of essential oil of lavender.

Herbal Vinegar

Chop 1 cup of selected herbs, pack loosely into a wide-mouth jar, and pour 1 pint of white vinegar to cover the herbs. Stir contents to release any air bubbles, seal, and let stand at room temperature for 10 to 12 days. If the finished product is too pungent for your taste, dilute with additional vinegar.

taught her. "I remember the pleasure of looking at plants and eating warm cherry tomatoes right from the vine. My daughters garden, too, but they don't like tomatoes. I like to think our love of gardening has been handed down through the generations, but somehow my love of sweet, ripe tomatoes wasn't inherited by my daughters."

Of course, we all enjoy some vegetables and fruits more than others, but it is interesting how childhood memories play such a part in forming our tastes and habits as adults. Mary Jo grew up on a farm in upstate New York. She remembers one crop she didn't like much as a child—rhubarb. "Even stewed with masses of sugar, the bitterness was more than the average kid can relate to. With time, though, I came to enjoy the bittersweet tang of rhubarb-and-strawberry pie or stewed rhubarb over ice cream—or even rhubarb spooned, cool and slippery, from a refrigerated bowl on a hot day." The years passed, and Mary Jo left home, entered college, and went on to her own life. The spring she bought her first house, she visited her parents' farm. On impulse, she asked to take a chunk of one of the rhubarb plants back to her new home. She planted the rhubarb in a corner of the yard, where it flourished. Mary Jo always appreciated this living connection to her childhood home.

Although my interest in gardening has been indulged mostly with indoor plants, my daughter is an avid outdoor gardener. She loves nothing better than spending hours outside tending to her flower and vegetable gardens. She didn't grow up having a vegetable garden, but like Deborah, a university professor who also knits and weaves, she has one now. Actually, Deborah's six-year-old daughter, Sarah, is part of her gardening team: "I love it when Sarah helps me harvest the veggies because she's so meticulous. She is very careful and asks questions about what is ready to be harvested, which plants are weeds, and what the rabbits would like to eat. We talk about what we're going to plant next year, if we should enlarge the garden, spread the rabbit droppings in the soil before winter or wait until spring planting. It's such a thoughtful, relaxed time for us to spend together."

Victory Gardens

During World War II, nearly 20 million Americans planted Victory Gardens. Public service booklets were published to teach the basics of gardening and soil health, including how, when, and what to plant in different areas of the country. This movement placed a strong emphasis on making gardening a family and community effort. In time, those gardens produced 40 percent of all the food that was consumed in this country.

Julia was born in 1935 and remembers very well when everyone had a Victory Garden. "Many foods were rationed, and anything that could be grown in small gardens in the back yard was either done by the family or in groups of several families together. Usually it fell to the women to do the gardens. Men were either at work, looking for work, or in the war. My mother was raised in Alabama and knew all about gardening from her mother. My grandmother not only had her own 'kitchen' garden, but fields of corn, potatoes, beans, sweet potatoes, and all kinds of melons. And there were the fruit and nut trees, too, all of them brimming with peaches, pears, and pecans. Mother grew up with a wonderful understanding of how to get the most and best from whatever amount of gardening space you had.

"I marveled more at the size of seeds as they were planted into the earth than at anything else. After they'd grown and made more vegetables, it just seemed like a wonderful magic trick. I still think about that. The speed at which we can see the results from seeds being planted and growing into something so good to eat is a miracle that all children can see and enjoy. Since I was allowed to help my mother with all of it, I found this to be especially true. Even today, I still find it gratifying to plant and grow things."

You might not have a lot of space, like Julia, but you can still grow plants for fresh, fragrant salads in containers on your patio or terrace. Container veggies need a rich soil mix, plenty of room for root growth, regular watering, and fertilizing. This is a project that teaches daughters of any age to choose which vegetables to grow and how to care for and harvest the plants that will make a fresh and nutritious salad. Here are just a few vegetables that have been bred for compact growth and small size:

- *Tomatoes*
- *Green onions*
- *Lettuce*
- *Chard*
- *Cucumbers*
- *Sweet peppers*
- *Baby carrots*

Today, people garden for a variety of reasons. Some prefer the superior taste of hours-old produce to what is available in grocery stores. Others garden because they want pesticide-free fruits and vegetables, or because they believe the act of gardening teaches valuable lessons. Regardless of the reasons it exists, a garden of any kind has a particularly calming quality at the end of the day and can be a place of refuge and reflection, no matter where we live and whatever our age. Whether you grow a single orchid, potted herbs on the patio, rows of vegetables, or an orange grove, follow these guidelines and introduce the tradition of gardening into your life—and share that tradition with your mother or daughter.

- *If you're a novice to gardening and have room for an outdoor garden, the first step is to take a mother/daughter tour of your neighborhood. Notice which shrubs, trees, and flowers are planted most often, how they're arranged, and what blooms from month to month. Chances are, people have selected these plants, and put them where they are, because they've had success with these conditions. Take a page from their book and duplicate what you already know works well.*

- *With the right plants and a few feeders, you can attract hummingbirds to your backyard or patio. These tiny birds can spot red from hundreds of feet away, so plant red flowers or tie red bows on tree branches. You can also buy specially designed feeders and fill them with four parts boiled water to one part sugar, as an extra incentive for these beautiful creatures to visit. Daughters of all ages will have fun with this project.*

- *Add an educational dimension to your garden by becoming an expert on just one plant. Roses, African violets, and orchids come in a variety of colors and are easy to care for. If you're worried about getting <u>any</u> plant to grow, try cacti. They come in an endless variety, including those that bloom.*

- *If you and your mother would like to discover and tour gardens open to the public, three hundred of them have been beautifully photographed in* National Geographic Guide to America's Public Gardens. *History, highlights, and hours of operation are included.*

- *The bookstore is full of books on gardening, but you might want to start out with magazines. Here are a few that I find helpful:* Herb Companion, Garden Design, Horticulture, Organic Gardening, *and* Kitchen Gardener.

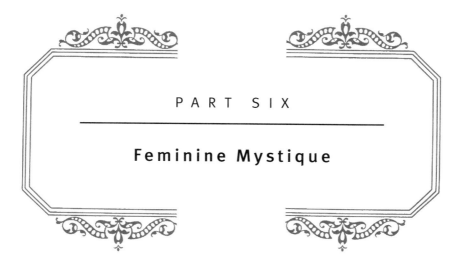

PART SIX

Feminine Mystique

Chapter 20

Best Friends

It's been said that one of the most difficult and important relationships in a woman's life is her relationship to her mother. As in all relationships, in this one the good times are coupled with the difficult. Most of us have both loved and hated our mothers, cherished and resented them, needed them desperately and wished they'd let us live our own lives. When things are going well, we feel comforted, supported, and loved, and when times are rough between moms and daughters, we can feel desperate and alone.

Although some young women use their mothers as a sounding board and a measure of themselves in both the best and worst of times, other daughters rebel and test their mother's resolve instead of being the perfect examples of what they want them to be. Sometimes the relationship is as easy as breathing, and sometimes we really have to work at it. At some point in their lives, though, our daughters become the individuals they want to be, and eventually we gain an understanding and acceptance of each other. That's when we achieve the balance that heralds the next step in our relationship—that of becoming best friends.

How do you go about being friends with your daughter? The best advice I can give you is to start at the beginning. When she's little, let her play dress-up in your clothes, put her artwork on the refrigerator, and buy anything she has to sell for school or church. As she grows older, encourage her to try new endeavors and let her know you believe in her. Praise her, even if she fails, and celebrate every victory, no matter how small. Last, don't forget to share *your* successes and failures with her so she'll always know she isn't alone.

Mommy's Little Girl

One thing you always do with your best friend is have fun. That's something Amy does with her three-year-old daughter, Liz: "Liz does play on her own and has a wonderful imagination, but I try to have some kind of really quality one-on-one time with her every day. One night last week we painted together. I have big plastic bottles of paint that I squirted out into stripes on paper plates to use as a palette. We used some small sponge shapes that my mom bought for Liz. She had great fun, even if her hands were gray for two days.

"Liz also loves to be read to, maybe because I began reading to her before she was born. My husband bought a bunch of Dr. Seuss books when I was pregnant and used to read them to my belly. I think the singsong rhythm of those books really helped when I read to her while she was nursing. And as she got older, as soon as I finished with one book, she was off to get another before I was able to get up from the chair. This Saturday we had a marathon reading day. We tried to read all the books on her shelf. That was fun until I got a sore throat, but a little hot tea and we were back in business. We never did get through all of her storybooks, but that's a challenge for another day. Everything I do, I do because I want Liz to grow up and know she is loved, always. I want her to try new things and learn as much as she can so that no matter what path she chooses in life, she will be happy. I hope that what I am doing now will help our relationship remain strong as she gets older."

Amy understands that it's never too early to sow the seeds of friendship with your daughter and do things together that are fun. I remember taking my daughter to the playground when she was little and instead of pushing her on the swings, I got on one next to her and pushed off toward the sky. I climbed on the monkey bars, played kick ball and "Mother May I." In case you think I felt silly, you'd be wrong. Having a little girl *with* me gave me the excuse to act like one, and I loved it. Here are some books that will give you great ways to be your daughter's playmate as well as her mom: *365 Days of Creative Play: For Children 2 Yrs. & Up,* by Judith Gray; *1001 Things to Do with Your Kids,* by Caryl Waller Krueger; and *Backyards and Butterflies: Ways to Include Children with Disabilities in Outdoor Activities,* by Doreen Greenstein.

If you're not the athletic type, take a tip from Doreen, a Girl Scout leader in her early thirties. Doreen has fond memories of her mother sharing "pretend games" with her and her sister when they were small. "I remember having tea parties when I was only three or four years old. My sister and I would get all gussied up and push our dolls in their carriages to the end of the driveway and then back to the house as though we were visiting. My mother would invite us and our babies in for tea and cookies." Doreen's mother took advantage of an opportunity to spend the afternoon *playing* with her daughters. We occasionally forget that this is an important part of teaching them.

More Than One Daughter

If you have more than one daughter, be sure to spend time with each of them—alone. Togetherness is good, but everyone needs individual attention. Doreen continues: "When I got older, my mother went to work. It was a change for us all because we no longer got to spend as much time with her. In order to give each of her children some one-on-one time, Mom started a tradition that is now shared by my daughter and me. Each Saturday, she would take one of us children to breakfast at Denny's before she started her shift. It was our time alone with her, and we each waited with great anticipation for the three weeks to go by for our next breakfast date with Mom. We would just sit at the restaurant and talk and simply be alone with my mother for an hour and a half. It was the most important thing in our lives at that time."

Doreen now lives a thousand miles away from her mother, but they still talk almost every day: "We share the day-to-day cares and problems of our lives. We talk about everything, and she listens just as she did when I was young, and shares those stories about life when I was three, six, and ten. I remember how she always listened as if the things we told her upon returning home from school were more important than anything else in the world to her. I believe they were and still are."

Tammy also has two daughters, Desiree, eleven, and Katelynn, nine. Tammy does most things with both girls, but sets aside one day a month to take each of them shopping and out to lunch. The time alone gives them the opportunity to talk and just be together. There's no competing for Mom's attention or arguing over who gets to pick where they go. I would suggest that you make the day special by slowing your pace for a few hours and choosing a sit-down restaurant, or plan monthly baking days with each girl when you can combine spending time together with teaching basic cooking skills.

Grade School Days

School days are filled with opportunities for mothers to be friends with young daughters. Phyllis lives in a small Eskimo community in Alaska, where the winters are long, dark, and cold. Although the school is only two blocks from home, Phyllis always walks with six-year-old Emily, who was adopted from China when she was a toddler. "We use our flashlights because it's not light until 11 A.M., and we hold hands. Sometimes we sing or I ask her to spell the spelling words for the week. We talk about the loose dogs and a wandering fox, and I tell her that she is safe with me and I'll scare them away." Phyllis is truly building the foundation of friendship with Emily. Just as Phyllis remembers feeling close to her mother when she was small, and always knowing she'd be there for whatever Phyllis needed, she's continuing the tradition by passing it on to Emily.

My father was in the air force, and we lived in Alaska when I was thirteen. I remember walking to the school bus stop, and it being so cold my eyes would tear up. I was too old to want my mother to walk to school with me, but I do remember the beautiful, deep red velvet parka she made me. It was patterned after the ones worn by Native Alaskan Eskimos, edged in silver trim and topped by a hood lined in rabbit fur. I guess you could say that my mother's love kept me warm every day.

Group Activities

I'm sure you've heard of the Take Your Daughter to Work Day, which has become a national tradition. A yarn shop in Campbell, California, tried a variant of that concept and held a Bring Your Daughter to Knit Day for its customers. The idea was to make knitting as special and social for daughters as it was for moms. Constance had taught her seven-year-old daughter, Erin, the basics of knitting, so they decided to attend.

"We arrived somewhat early, so we went to a restaurant to have breakfast. Erin was delighted to have private time with me and excited about the upcoming knitting adventure. There ended up being three women and five children there—Barbara and her six-year-old, Claire, Carol and her ten-year-old daughter and her two friends, me, and Erin. It was pleasantly low-key. The younger two knit for a while and then left for the more entrancing game of picking small scraps of yarn and random bits of fluff from the store's fine collection of fleeces and roving. I like that my daughter enjoys going to the yarn store with me. Part of her pleasure is the focused time with me, and part is that she becomes part of a larger circle of interesting women who admire her efforts. To me, it feels like taking part in a time-honored ritual. Someday she'll be teaching her daughter to knit and praising her efforts, just as I have with her."

You can create a mother/daughter friendship circle and get together once a week. Try to get away from distractions by going for a walk, sipping tea on the patio, or sharing the privacy of your bedroom or den. Talk about your dreams and everything else that comes to mind, whether it's school, work, fashion, or fun.

Stand-In Moms

Some daughters have a woman in their lives who fills the shoes of their mom but who isn't—biologically speaking. That might give this "mom" a somewhat easier time of being a best friend. Tammy, who has five daughters, had her Aunt Orie to act as her mentor: "She was a rather quiet lady—a little introverted and always in the shadow of her more vocal sisters. She definitely spoiled me. I knew it and she did, too. Together, it was our secret conspiracy. Aunt Orie was criticized that she 'didn't make me mind.' She listened to her sisters' protests, then quietly went on and did exactly as she pleased with me. Somewhere, in a childhood memory, I can still hear the squeak of her oak rocker while I spent countless hours on her lap while she read me stories. She kept my books and toys in the window seat, and occasionally I would open it to find something new. We were special buddies, and I only hope that I can pass on to my children a little of the enormous gifts she gave to me."

Teenage Years

Joanne is a stay-at-home mom to Jacquelyn, fifteen. When Joanne was growing up, her father traveled quite a bit on business, so she and her mother did everything together. "She treated me much the same way as she would any other friend, and I grew up knowing I could confide in her about anything. In my teen years we were as close as ever, and we'd often go out for a shopping trip and a chocolate shake, or just for a ride somewhere. Because of the relationship I had with my mom, I've always treated Jacquelyn the same way. From the time she was a toddler I'd talk to her about everything. I don't think there was a time I ever talked down to her because she was a child, and I've always respected her as a person. She's grown into a wonderful young woman, and we really enjoy spending time together. We have many of the same interests, including baking, antiques, tea parties, history, and just laughing together."

Joanne believes that a mom can be best friends with her teenage daughter if she bonds with her child early. "You can't wait until your child is in her teens to try to establish a friendly relationship. By then it's too late, and there have been too many other outside influences. You have to let them know from the time they're babies and toddlers that you not only love them but that you like and respect them, as well."

Another important thing to remember is that there may be times when your teenage daughter will not act like she wants to be friends with you. Keep in mind that she's confused about life and her place in the world. That's only natural. She doesn't know who she is, and she's desperately afraid of becoming her mother. This is when you have to remain confident that she'll come back to you once she's figured things out. If you remain connected, she'll come to understand that emulating you isn't so bad after all and that she wants you to be part of her life.

Doreen's teenage years were tumultuous for both her and her mother. "I was the oldest, and we were both new to the experience, so my mother and I lost touch as I approached adulthood. We didn't talk or see each other for quite some time after I left home. I have never asked her how she handled it, because I feel so guilty about putting her through so much hell. However, things began to change shortly before the birth of my daughter. Throughout most of my pregnancy, I was not in contact with my family, but toward the end we reunited. The night I delivered my daughter, Mom was with me. She held my hand and talked to me. She wiped my forehead and brought me ice chips. My mother was there to see my daughter enter this world, and it was such a miraculous thing for her to be able to see *her* baby deliver a baby. I couldn't have imagined how much comfort my mother would give to me during those few hours."

When I first heard Doreen's story, I knew why her mother was able to get past whatever difficulties had been put between them. A mother's love for her daughter is probably the strongest bond possible between two people. Not that a mother can or should condone everything her teenager does—but the day will come when the past is just that, the past. I think the same holds true for daughters. Sometimes it's the mother who is difficult, and at some point in their lives, daughters are also able to forge a new, adult relationship with the most important woman in their lives.

There are so many changes and thoughts going through a teenage daughter's mind that they can sometimes seem aloof, disinterested, or too busy to spend time with Mom. Don't let that stop you. Carve time out of both her busy schedule and your own, even if it's only minutes on the clock. Remember, there's no way for her to confide in you if you're not available. Remember, too, that you *can* have a meaningful conversation over morning coffee or right before she goes to bed.

When I asked Fran, a novelist, to comment on the difficulties between mothers and teenage daughters, she commented, "There seems to be a natural separation process that occurs during those years. Later, and usually after a daughter has left home and been on her own for a while, she'll pick up the best of her mother's traits and try to carry them on. Some mothers handle this process better than others. I was lucky that I was never so angry with my mother, or she with me, that it caused a serious rift between us. Many women I know either don't speak to their mothers or don't get along with them. These women date their estrangement back to their angst-ridden teen years because their mothers made them feel they didn't live up to their expectations."

Adult Daughters

The public relationship between country singers Naomi and Wynonna Judd represents the dynamic bond that links mothers to their adult daughters. Together, they pursued a career and shared both the difficulties and rewards as partners. Although they apparently experienced some turbulence in their relationship when Wynonna was growing up, they always shared common interests and goals. That certainly helped pave the way for their close professional partnership. But I think their close *personal* relationship—one that helped conquer Naomi's bout with hepatitis C and the tabloids' pursuit of Wynonna—is what gave them the strength and fortitude to make their dreams come true.

Valerie has been blessed with both a lovely daughter and a daughter-in-law who also has a wonderful relationship with her mother. "We all know marriage and motherhood come with many 'how to' books and magazine articles nowadays, but in earlier times, young women lacked the knowledge that we take for granted. There were no talk shows and trendy magazine quizzes to help you choose the right mate or raise the next genius baby. They didn't have the Internet to plug into chat groups, share ideas, and ask questions of noted doctors in their field of great expertise. More often than not, these young women looked to their own mothers as role models.

"My daughter, Amy, seems to be relaxed and capable after only her first year of marriage. I can sense how little she needs my advice, and my confidence in her gives me an overwhelming feeling of pride and happiness. As mothers, we should all be assured our daughters will learn from our example and that they will do just fine out in the world."

You'll probably want to be your daughter's best friend in everything that she does, especially when she falls in love, marries, and starts to think about creating the next generation of your family. Here are a few suggestions for mothers and daughters of all ages who want to be best friends:

- *Take lessons together—yoga, tennis, golf, painting, or anything that strikes both of you as interesting and fun.*
- *Volunteer as docents at an art museum or zoo.*
- *Check with your local library to see if it has a mother/daughter book club. If it doesn't, start one of your own. A good resource is* The Mother-Daughter Book Club: How Ten Busy Mothers and Daughters Came Together to Talk, Laugh and Learn Through Love of Reading, *by Shireen Dodson.*
- *If you have a young daughter, make a "play date" every week for just the two of you. Go to a neighborhood park or a grade school playground and play on the swings, climb the monkey bars, play tag, or build sand castles.*
- *Invite your mother or daughter out for an afternoon luncheon. Choose a quiet restaurant with a view, one that features wonderful music or serves a scrumptious afternoon tea. Talk, listen, and get reacquainted.*
- *Grown-up daughters, invite your mothers for a weekend retreat at a spa. Treat yourselves to a facial, hair conditioning, a new cut or color, and a massage. It's a great way to spend time together and relax.*

Chapter 21

Feminine Nature

We want our daughters to grow up to be emotionally and physically strong individuals. At the same time, we want to show them how to embrace their feminine nature and learn to become the women we know they can be. Indeed, a girl with a strong sense of who she is and what she believes in has a better chance of making the choices that will move her along the path to becoming a confident, happy woman.

Many cultures celebrate and acknowledge a girl's coming-of-age with ceremonies such as the Latin Quinceañera, which takes place on a girl's fifteenth birthday. The Jewish tradition celebrates a girl's entrance into adulthood with a Bat Mitzvah at age thirteen or fourteen. The parents present their daughter with a prayer shawl, and the entire community recognizes her as a member of its adult society. Navajo people traditionally have a four-day ceremony honoring a girl's coming-of-age, after which she is considered to have acquired the "Changing Woman's" power to heal. Many tribes in Africa, Australian Aborigines, people in the Middle East, and many other cultures have important, ritualized rites of passage for young girls. Unfortunately, American culture seems to have lost many of the celebrations that mark life-changing passages.

In the face of that cultural loss, the mother/daughter relationship can be the bricks and mortar of a sturdy foundation that enables young women to build their feminine experience. Ultimately, teaching girls the importance of being female is something that only a woman can do. Karen grew up with a mother who was "observant and thought deeply about everything." There wasn't a question she couldn't ask, nor an answer that wouldn't be given. "When my mother talked about sex, menstruation, birth, nursing, and all things 'female,' I could tell that she delighted in being a woman and that the awe and pleasure of that experience brought her wonderment at the mysteries of life."

If you have a young daughter, consider how best to explain the physical and emotional changes of puberty, and don't leave the details of this important transformation to chance. If you're not sure what to do or say, there are dozens of books available, and although books can be a good source of information, nothing can compare or comfort more than a good mother-to-daughter talk.

Oral Tradition

Many cultures have a history of oral tradition in which elders pass on stories to their children. Jeannie, a farm wife and naturalist, remembers her mother instilling in her a strong sense of honor. "Our family has been in the United States since the late 1600s, and while I was growing up my mother told me many stories about the brave men and women in our family. That verbal tradition has a lot to do with who I am today, and I value those stories for the richness they bring to my life. Over the years, I've retold the stories my mother told me to my daughter, Carrie." Feminine nature isn't just the physical and emotional side of the spirit—it includes character, courage, and honor. Like Jeannie's mother, we can pass that tradition to our daughters, too.

Women's Roles

Today, women are oftentimes confused about the difference and the similarities between men and women. Roles aren't as clearly defined as they once were, and we are struggling to discover just where we fit into our world. When Mara was a young girl, she wasn't interested in baking, sewing, or any craft activities. Her mother had been reared in a family with old-fashioned ideas about the role of women in society, and she was determined to raise Mara quite differently. Mara was taught to believe she could do or be anything she chose.

Once she married and had two daughters, Mara began to see things in a new light. "I now realize what a wonderful gift it is to have children. I think I'm doing the most important job in the world, as did my mother and her mother before her. I realize that being a feminist is supporting women in whatever their choices in life may be. My mother gave me a precious gift by being at home to raise me, and I'd like to give this same gift to my daughters."

Public opinion has vacillated about whether or not mothers should stay at home with their children. Women have been made to feel guilty for going to work, and other times they've felt slighted for staying home. Fortunately, women today seem to make decisions based on their own values, abilities, goals, and circumstances rather than current public mores. The increase of home-based businesses has given women have even more opportunities to be at home with their children.

The Feminine Side

Lynnette is in her early thirties and a stay-at-home mom. Her seven-year-old daughter, Abigail, always chooses to see the glass half full instead of half empty. She continually tells her mommy how beautiful she is or how lovely the house looks. Even though Abigail also does things quite differently from her mother, Lynnette has adopted her daughter's attitude of seeing the positive rather than the negative. When Abigail chooses to wear mismatched hair barrettes or Mom's least favorite skirt, Lynnette never criticizes. Instead, she tells Abigail how proud she is that she combed her hair or chose to wear a dress. Abigail will learn what colors and patterns go together someday, but for now "she just needs to know that Mommy approves of her desire to look nice."

Bathing

From the time your daughter is born, you can make bath time a special, enjoyable experience for both of you. Use fragrant soaps, bubble bath crystals, lotion, talcum powder, and big fluffy towels. Relax, take your time, and start a tradition filled with intimacy. Once a girl reaches puberty, she might want more privacy, and her wishes should be respected. There are still a few times when you can make a bath a mother/daughter ritual:

- *When she's ready to first shave her underarms and legs*
- *When she's getting ready for a party or outing*
- *When you are getting ready for a special occasion*

Encourage your daughter to enjoy her bath, no matter whether she's two years old or twenty. Lend or buy her bubble bath, scented soaps and powders, and bath oils. You might even take her shopping to choose her own feminine toiletries.

Mistie juggles her roles as wife, mother, and college student, while still finding time to share her feminine side with five-year-old daughter Alexis. Her husband is periodically away from home for days, sometimes longer. Instead of focusing on the separation, Mistie uses this time to strengthen her relationship with her daughter. Alexis "loves to do things like Mommy," so Mistie regularly schedules a "girls' night" when Daddy is out of town, and the time is spent doing whatever Alexis wants. "We take a bath together and use 'moldable foamy soap' to spray the shapes of necklaces and bracelets on each other. After the bath, we usually move into my bedroom to watch cartoons while I paint Alexis's fingernails. I'm so happy to be able to spend this time with her. It gives me a chance to see Alexis as a growing little girl, and gives her a chance to see that being with Mommy can be fun."

One year, my daughter, Heather, gave me a unique and very feminine gift for my birthday. She'd gone to a shop that offers a special service—creating a perfume based on personality and favorite scents from nature and beyond. I love roses, vanilla, and the misty rain of springtime. Heather's creativity and attention to detail went into that special scent, and I'll always remember that gift from the heart. Femininity is truly what you make of it. Calming, delicious, invigorating, sensuous, and pleasurable fun can be brought about by trying out scents, makeup, creams, lotions, fingernail polish, and new hairstyles.

Hair Grooming

One of my favorite movies is *Little Women,* adapted from the book by Louisa May Alcott. Scenes from the movie show a loving Marmee brushing her daughters' hair and the daughters grooming each other. Yet, they remind me that, unfortunately, feminine nurturing seems to be missing in our modern, hectic lives.

Teaching your daughter how to care for and style her hair not only shows your respect for her desire to be attractive, it also gives you time to be alone with her. Barbara, an author, has a special daily ritual with her daughter, Kristen. Barbara's mother always kept Barbara's hair short, so Barbara has always let Kristen wear hers long. In the evenings, Kristen will bring the hairbrush to Barbara so she can comb out all the tangles before bedtime. Then in the morning, Kristen helps her mom decide how she will wear her hair. Barbara wants Kristen to be able to express her feminine nature however she chooses—even with her hairstyle.

If your daughter is grown or your mother is elderly, you can still share and celebrate feminine values by going to the hair salon together. For extra pampering, have a deep conditioning treatment. If your mother is ill, you can cheer her immensely by washing, setting, and brushing out her hair just the way she likes it.

Cosmetics

Cosmetics might hold a particular allure for today's young girls and women, but face painting is an age-old tradition for both men *and* women. Egyptian tombs are lined with drawings and statues with kohl-ringed eyes. Native American, African, and Australian tribes have a generations-long tradition of painting their faces and bodies for special ceremonies. Face and body adornment have held special significance for centuries, and today's young girls experiment with cosmetics for an important reason, too. They want to change the way they look. When a girl takes this step, she's also making a statement that symbolizes an ancient rite of passage. She's stepping out of the role of little girl into adulthood.

Some mothers try to forbid this transformation, especially when the mom feels her daughter is too young for makeup. Although a mother might be justified in some cases, I think the better route is to encourage a daughter's experimentation—even if it is allowed only at home. A young girl will try on many different "faces" during her teenage years, using cosmetics, hairstyles, clothing, and behavior. This is a necessary and healthy part of growing up. Experience it along with your daughter, and help her with tips and advice, rather than just saying no.

I clearly remember being thirteen or fourteen and putting on lipstick and eyeliner *after* I left the house. When short skirts were in style, my mother wouldn't let me wear them, so I simply rolled my waistband up a few inches. If you rear a girl to be strong-minded, she's likely to be that in all things, including her appearance. It's important that you nurture a positive self-image in your daughter. Give her your acceptance and provide a safe, secure place for her to explore who she is and who she wants to be. It can make all the difference in her life.

Take your daughter shopping and let her choose a few cosmetics for herself. This will also give you the opportunity to talk about *removing* makeup, as well as how to keep her skin clean and deal with blemishes. Help her choose appropriate products for those needs, too.

Clothing and Wardrobes

Buying or making clothes is a wonderful mother/daughter tradition, especially when it comes to school clothes. The beginning of a new school year is an opportunity to celebrate that your daughter is growing older, as well as a chance to introduce her to both the fashion and function of clothing. Here are some ways to begin fostering your daughter's fashion consciousness:

- *Start by going through her closet <u>with her</u>, discarding anything that's beyond repair or no longer fits.*
- *Once you have a clear idea of what you have to start with, you can sit down together to decide what she needs and wants.*
- *Make a list. You probably won't stick to it completely, but it will make shopping easier and ensure that you don't forget something important.*
- *Help your daughter choose clothing and accessories, but don't insist on buying something you like but she doesn't. Generally, those items are pushed to the back of the closet and never worn anyway.*

Taking your daughter to buy her first bra is another adolescent ritual. You can measure her, show her how to choose the right size, and explain the advantages of different styles and fabrics. This might seem simple to you, but it is a whole new world for your daughter. Wearing a bra is a sign that she is one step closer to becoming a woman. Celebrate with her and welcome her with open arms into the big girls' club.

Dressing up in Mom's clothes is another method of exploration for your daughter. I don't remember playing dress-up with my mother's clothes, but our next-door neighbor, Lucy, was the next best thing. She occasionally baby-sat my sister and me, and she quickly figured out how to keep us entertained—she let us play dress-up. Lucy had dozens of pretty nightgowns in a palette of colors and styles, and a dizzying array of costume jewelry and high heels. She would help us choose our costumes and, once we were dressed, pour 7-Up into champagne glasses and make a toast to the grown-up ladies.

Nurturing

We all have different ideas of what mothers do and how they should care for their children. Karen believes our notions usually come from our own experience: "My oldest daughter, Eva, used to worry that she wouldn't be a good mother because she couldn't core apples exactly the way I could, and that seemed like an important motherly skill to her. She also mentioned that spreading butter (peanut butter or jam) clear to the edges of the bread was something only a mother would do, and how that makes her feel well cared for. I think she must be remembering all the times she's watched me coring apples, making sandwiches, taking care of things for her, and has developed that into her idea of how a mother should nurture."

Doreen always knew her mother loved her because she showed it in so many ways. When she was sick, her mother always got up, no matter how late it was or how tired she might have been, and sat with her until she went back to sleep. Her mother always listened to the things Doreen and her sister told her when they returned home from school: "We were always the number one thing in her life, and we still are."

Luckily for Doreen, she never had to wonder if her mother cared. "When there were serious issues to be discussed, Mom would make us each a cup of tea and we would sit together at the kitchen table and talk. One time, Mom found out that my sister and I had taken a couple of my father's cigarettes and given them a try. She sat us at the table with our tea and we talked about why we'd done that. She never got upset or screamed. She always remained calm and comforting. In years to come, we felt very comfortable going to her with problems most girls never discussed with their mothers. I'm sure it was never easy for her to hear some things, but she always listened and I always felt she helped me." Over the years, Doreen and her mother have become close friends. They talk just about every day, and share the routine cares and problems of their lives.

The best way to encourage your daughter to explore her femininity is to spend time with her alone. Focus on helping her understand herself and her potential. Ask about her dreams, give her a strong foundation, and nurture her feminine spirit until she achieves whatever it is she wants to be. Feminine traditions should start at birth and be celebrated throughout a woman's life. If you've been standing on the sidelines, it's not too late to discover or renew this special aspect of the mother/daughter relationship. Here are some ways to take that first step:

- *Create or join a group of mothers and daughters who want to celebrate feminine values. Study different cultures around the world and discuss how to bring traditions into your life that honor the feminine spirit.*
- *Learn more about Gaia, Greek goddesses, and Mother Earth. These studies will help you explore ways in which you might intertwine spirituality with feminine nature.*
- *If your daughter has expressed an interest in a field you know little or nothing about, find her a female role model and mentor. If there's no one in your family or friendship circle, try co-workers, church members, women you see on a professional basis (doctors or lawyers, for example), or fraternal organizations.*
- *If you don't have a positive body image, think back to your childhood for clues. If you feel your mother didn't understand how you felt or who you were, determine to change things with your young daughter.*

Chapter 22

Honor Your *Self*

*D*o you remember as a child writing your name over and over again, as if trying to "see" who you were, make sense of yourself, or make yourself real? Honoring your *self* is remembering the best part of who you are and who you've become through your personal journey of discoveries. We need to continue along that road throughout life if we are to realize our full potential and discover the dreams hidden deep inside—the ones we're too shy to say out loud and sometimes are afraid to try. We must live our lives with the right perspective, priorities, and relationships in order to both open and close the doors that present themselves to us. As we become better connected with our selves, we might have more questions than answers, but if we listen carefully the answers will come, along with a renewed sense of purpose and identity.

Finding Your Passion

It's not nearly as difficult as you might think. All of us need to keep an open mind about the possibilities, and focus on our heart's desire without the fear of letting go. If you're like most people, you keep on doing what you're doing not for the love of it but because the fear of losing money and security, or of trying something new, is stronger than your desires. The best way to face these fears is to look in the mirror and tell yourself that the most precious things in the world aren't silver and gold but what's felt with the heart. If, at the end of your workday, you ask yourself, "What's the point?" perhaps you need to re-evaluate what's holding you back from doing something you find meaningful. Instead of belaboring that point while you're soul-searching and researching some of your ideas, stay focused on the passion, not the fear. You might want to:

- *Think back about the things you truly have loved doing in your life. What games did you like as a child? What hobbies do you enjoy? What jobs fulfilled you personally—jobs that you would have done regardless of pay?*
- *Do some soul-searching and personal development work by making lists, reading books, and talking to people.*
- *Ask yourself, "What are my unique talents and gifts?" This is important, because if we find a way to use our gifts to the fullest, we will love doing that work.*
- *Explore the job opportunities that would allow you to use those gifts and pursue your interests. If you can't think of any, you can create one yourself.*

Rita finished college and went directly into the workforce. However, after a few years she found that the more money she made, the less time she had to enjoy it. The path she had chosen didn't inspire her, and it didn't make her want to jump out of bed every morning, either. She tried to find her passion by doing some of what I've suggested—writing lists of interests and reading books. She even took a couple of jobs she thought might be interesting, only to become discouraged and quit within a few weeks. "It was only when I opened myself up to the gift of a 'blank page' that I was able to find hope for the future," Rita says. "You see, working with a blank page means you're open to opportunities and choices. You might write a few lines one day and erase them the next. You can choose, or not, and you can change your mind one day and your life the next."

I agree with Rita that we need to be open to new ideas and opportunities, but I think we also have to acknowledge another truth—that *not* choosing is in itself a choice. It's not a good idea to go through life trying one thing, then another, without ever committing to a purpose and plan of action. We are, after all, setting examples for our daughters. Sometimes we have to follow our heart's desire while getting up and going to work somewhere else. You can do both and still honor your *self*.

Age-Old Advice

Marlene, a textile artist, discovered that many of the age-old sayings her mother used profusely when she was a child were lessons that helped her along the road to finding her passion.

"*If a thing is worth doing, it is worth doing well.* This lesson was in reference to my sloppy sewing of a pocket on the inside of a jacket. When I complained that no one would ever see it, my mother repeated this saying and went into great detail on why it should matter to me. Since then, I have used that old saying to call forth the best that is in me.

"*A stitch in time saves nine.* I apply this saying to many things besides sewing and feel fortunate that my mother encouraged me to explore many interests. She helped me to see the value of following my dreams and that my attempts at new things were worthy endeavors."

Strength and Spirit

Doreen has a thirteen-year-old daughter and describes herself as being "on the twenty-year plan" to get her bachelor's degree. The person who had the most influence on her was her mom. "Her strength and spirit is something I've always admired. When I was a child, it was the way she colored—always staying in the lines and using beautiful colors to create masterpieces compared to my pictures. She always said mine were beautiful, but I knew they weren't. Now that I have a daughter, I understand my mother was really encouraging me to try, helping me to feel good about myself. Many years have gone by, and both our lives have changed. Where I admired her for small things as a child, I now admire her strength and spirit. Some years ago, a terrible accident left my mother a paraplegic. Although this was a horrible experience, she is a stronger person than many people could ever hope to be. That's where I find an indestructible inner strength when I need it most."

Jeannie has the same description for her daughter, Carrie: "One of the great joys of my life is my daughter. She has done well in her life, and it is a source of pride for me that she has been so successful. It is hard for a parent to let go of a child, but she is living proof that I've taught her well. I made a lot of mistakes, too, but I have also given her strength and will. I'm proud of that. I never really realized how much of what my mother knew was passed on to me, but now Carrie and my younger sister are both asking *me* the questions. How strange it seems to be stepping into the role of matriarch of our little family group. I hope they look to me because of the strength I've gained over the years."

Mother Isn't My Name

When a mother has a strong identity, her daughter learns that it's "okay to be me." It's important for women to establish their own identities with their children and encourage them to have interests of their own. But in order to honor our *selves,* we have to remember that our own name is so much more than "Mother."

Mara has two daughters and is currently studying naturopathy. When she was growing up, she shared a love of animals with her mother. "My mother was always so good with the animals. We had dogs and cats, hamsters and goldfish, and my mom and I had our horses. We would go on long trail rides together, and I can still feel the breeze in my hair and the sun beating down on me as we rode up the riverbed. Mom didn't like to run the horses as much as I did, but sometimes we would race up a hill on the return home. We worked together, too, mucking out the corral and hauling home bales of hay from the feed store. We spent long afternoons brushing the horses and digging out the rocks in their hooves. I think this was really a time of freedom that my mother and I could share, doing something we both loved and appreciated. It also helped me to see my mother as a *person* and not just my mother."

When You're Adopted

Jenn found that being adopted can affect the way people see themselves while they are growing up. She has only come to terms with her identity and her family in the last few years.

"Family, heritage, and tradition are words that are powerful. For me, though, these words have helped me to both belong and not belong. I've known that I was adopted for as long as I've been aware of my *self*. It's not as though there's anything wrong with being adopted—many of my best friends are, which suggests that adoption is a central part of my identity.

"I remember how upset my sister was when I started looking for my birth parents, how afraid she was that I would find out I had a 'real' sister and that I wouldn't love her anymore. And I remember the sudden understanding in that moment, the recognition that 'family' had nothing to do with shared blood but rather with shared experiences, love, and history. Those two concurrent stories, the two sides of my adoption, are always there, and without them I would be someone else entirely.

"My grandmother was a big part of our lives growing up, and every time she visited, she brought special food that only she made. Wedges of sandwiches, the fillings precisely minced and mixed, tomato aspic with Miracle Whip salad dressing as a garnish, and baking—especially her pink cake. The recipe had been lost and my grandmother gone for years, but recently the recipe resurfaced, and I determined to make that pink cake. Just looking at the recipe evoked so many memories. Not only was it written in Nana's handwriting, but there were little notes recorded all over it: next to the '½ cup flour' notation was a penciled 'try ⅓ generous.' Seeing how she had refined and perfected the recipe made it seem almost as though she were there in the kitchen with me, voicing these hints and suggestions to help me follow her path. However, even with her helpful notes, the cake didn't turn out right. It was too brown, the icing too pink, and it definitely wasn't the pink cake of my memory. When I expressed my frustration, Dad mentioned that Nana always used golden sugar. I checked, but the recipe said 'brown sugar,' not 'golden.' But he was sure, as was his brother. And so I tried again, and suddenly I had the pink cake. Even better, though, I also had a little note of my own to add to the recipe.

"And suddenly it all clicked for me. I looked through the battered shoe box that held family recipes and saw all sorts of handwriting: my grandmother's, my mom's, my dad's neat printing, my own much younger printing. That's when I added my own note to my grandmother's recipe. And then there was healing. I built a bridge between the solitudes of myself and linked the two stories of my life into a larger whole. And, most important, I found my own way into the family traditions from which I had felt estranged. The sense of tradition and heritage that I couldn't find resides in a battered shoe box in my mother's kitchen."

Loss of *Self*

As Jenn found her *self* through the power of traditions, Beth, at thirty, has already faced the loss of traditions through her mother's devastating disease, multiple sclerosis. "Her MS is somewhat unusual in that it has impaired her mind as much as her body in ways similar to Alzheimer's. In most ways, I think it might be easier to lose someone quickly than it is to have what they refer to as a 'long goodbye.' Sometimes I look back and try to figure out exactly when I lost her, but I'm not sure. When you lose your mother, you lose your model of how things should be done, and it's like having to forge your own path all the time instead of following a path. I remember how lost I felt when I got married, because my mother couldn't really participate. I would ask her about my dress or veil, and I just couldn't engage her emotionally.

"Now I have come to rely on my oldest sister. She's ten years older, so I've had a chance to watch her raise her children, and the traditions I do have, have come from her. Because I don't have many preconceived ideas about traditions, it's fun to read about and decide what traditions I'd like to establish as my own. Now that I have a daughter, I'm careful to document everything because I long for her to have the familiarity of traditions that I have missed. I want to leave a legacy behind so she'll have traditions that she can keep and help her feel that she has something of me. Coming from a family with few traditions, and having experienced so much loss, I think they are all the more important to me and help me feel grounded in a world where I no longer have my mother."

Traditions can be a pathway to that sense of self we've been talking about, and connecting with our innermost thoughts should be a priority. If you don't feel you're in touch with your self, or if you've just been so busy that you've gotten lost in the shuffle, it's time to reconnect. Here are some final thoughts on how you can revitalize your self:

- *Give yourself quiet time to allow for the stream of consciousness that can lead to a new perspective.*
- *Carve out a big enough block of time to get past your everyday concerns to really get to the core of what your spirit wants to tell you.*
- *Once you hear those thoughts, strive to be true and honest to your innermost beliefs and desires.*
- *Try waking up a half hour earlier in the morning, taking a walk by yourself in the evenings, or writing for half an hour in your personal journal.*

Final Thoughts

*T*raditions are a lifeline that carry the heart and soul of a family from one generation to the next. And, to a great degree, the responsibility for this lifeline has been entrusted to mothers. I decided to explore the link among mothers, daughters, and traditions because of my own experiences and those of women I know both personally and through E-mail lists on the Internet. As I listened to women talk and write about the traditions they learned from their mothers and handed down to their daughters, I came to a greater understanding of the importance of this connection between women.

I hope the stories, ideas, and inspirations in this book will carry into your own lives and those of your mothers and daughters. Remember, it's easy for traditions to be lost—all it takes is one generation to be too busy, or to forget. However, it's just as easy for traditions to be reclaimed. If traditions aren't a part of your life, create new ones or take a fresh look at those from the past and revitalize them. Keep in mind that it is through tradition—the power of knowledge, understanding, skill, artistry, and love—that we preserve the families of our daughters and granddaughters. Put your creativity and energy into nurturing your traditions, and chances are they will outlive you and carry your essence into generations to come.

During this personal journey, I have revisited my own memories and gained an even deeper respect for my own mother and mothers everywhere. I've enjoyed listening to my daughter tell stories from her childhood, too. The relationship between mother and daughter might be eternal, but sisters, nieces, godmothers, cousins, and your very dearest friends are also integral parts of your collective family. If we teach others what our mothers and grandmothers taught us, we will all complement each other's lives.

I hope you'll share the traditions presented in this book with all the women in your lives. Remember, too, that when we celebrate our memories, we honor the past and carry our traditions from one generation to the next—together.

© Heather Marlowe

About the Author

Joyce Marlow's love of arts and crafts began when her mother taught her to sew at age ten, and it has continued throughout her life. She especially enjoys textile and fiber arts, including weaving, spinning, knitting, needlepoint, and sewing. Joyce is currently Executive Director of a private nonprofit transitional center in rural Washington State, where she lives with her life partner and is shepherd to a small flock of sheep.